501

practical ways

to teach your children

values

Bobbie Reed, Ph.D.

SAINT LOUIS

To Holly,
for Alexandra,
with love

Scripture quotations marked KJV are from the King James or Authorized Version of the Bible.

Scripture quotations marked RSV are from the Revised Standard Version of the Bible, copyrighted 1946, 1952, © 1971, 1973 by the Division of Christian Education of the National Council of the Churches of Christ in the U.S.A., and are used by permission.

All Scripture quotations, unless otherwise indicated, are taken from the HOLY BIBLE, NEW INTERNATIONAL VERSION®. NIV®. Copyright © 1973, 1978, 1984 by International Bible Society. Used by permission of Zondervan Publishing House. All rights reserved.

Copyright © 1998 Concordia Publishing House
3558 S. Jefferson Avenue, St. Louis, MO 63118-3968
Manufactured in the United States of America

Library of Congress Cataloging-in-Publication Data

Reed, Bobbie
    501 practical ways to teach your children values / Bobbie Reed.
        p.   cm.
    ISBN 0-570-04994-6
    1. Christian education of children.   2. Values—Study and teaching.
    3. Children—Religious life.   I. Title.
    BV1475.2.R39   1998
    248.8'45–dc21   97-37079

1 2 3 4 5 6 7 8 9 10   07 06 05 04 03 02 01 00 99 98

Contents

how children learn values

> *"Darcy is just a joy," Doug said of his 17-year-old daughter. "She and I share about spiritual things. She has such a heart for God, and she actively shares her faith with her friends. Donna and I are not only proud of her and love her, we simply enjoy having her as our daughter. She has never given us grief."* Doug's eyes reflected his deep happiness and fulfillment as a dad.

NOT ALL PARENTS are as blessed as Donna and Doug. We sometimes experience joy, and we sometimes despair of ever getting through to our children. The moments when I've felt the most fulfilled as a parent have been when my sons showed signs of adopting one of my values or beliefs. Conversely, my deepest disappointments have been when they've chosen to reject important parts of my value system. The stronger our personal value system, the more compelled we feel to instill that same system in our children, particularly when our values spring from a firm faith in God.

However, values cannot be imposed or superimposed. They only can be communicated and taught. Each of us must choose what is valuable to us. The more you help your children see and experience a particular belief as personally valuable, the more likely they are to adopt it as their value.

What Are Values?

A value is a belief that, after careful consideration, has been selected from various choices and is acted upon repeatedly and consistently over a period of time. Sometimes values are identified by a single word such as "honesty" or described as a character trait such as "dependable." But the core value would actually be stated as a belief such as "It is right to be honest in all situations" or "I believe it is important to be dependable." We all have values.

Values help us evaluate and choose between alternatives and help us decide how to behave in a consistent manner. Without a clear set of values, our lives and our behaviors tend to be inconsistent and confusing. Imagine bringing to your city a Brazilian Indian who has never been away from his village. His village is located 400 miles from the nearest town, and no road exists to the outside world. He may not have the same set of values to help him behave as people do in your city. He might walk around almost naked, as he did in the jungle; kill any edible animal he saw for food (including neighborhood pets); eat his meals squatting on the floor; or build a fire in the backyard. He could not drive a car because he would have no concept of right of way, four-way stops, traffic lights, speed limits, or how to operate the vehicle. If he were determined to adjust to city living, he probably would be a willing student of whoever was willing to teach him. But he wouldn't learn everything at once. He wouldn't understand the importance of the many values, and he might adamantly refuse to accept some things as right. As he learned how things work best in your city, he would become less confused and his behavior would become more consistent with yours.

In some ways our children are like that Brazilian Indian. They start life without knowing how the world works or how to build healthy reciprocal relationships. They do not have a personal set of values, and initially they may develop conflicting values and beliefs that lead to inconsistencies and confusion. Part of growing up involves sorting through the conflicts and confusion and making new choices that eliminate the major clashes in values. In fact, even adults experience confusion and conflict until they establish congruent beliefs that provide order for areas of their lives such as politics, religion, family, friendships, work, leisure activities, love, sex, male/female roles, health, money, personal habits, education, and on and on!

Of course, there still can be conflicts when two good values seem to pull in opposing directions. If you know that a good friend is doing something illegal at work, do you keep quiet (loyalty) or report the offense (honesty)? Most children experience similar conflicts and probably won't tell on their friends. This book will not eliminate those kinds of conflicts. However, this book will help children understand their values so they can develop a code of conduct and make God-pleasing choices in difficult situations.

How Can Parents Teach Values?

As Christian parents, we look to God's Word and the loving example of Jesus, God's Son, when we share values with our children. Remember how the Spirit of Christ totally changed the apostle Paul's values? Before his experience on the Damascus road, Paul's values were based on achievements—a Pharisee, zealously persecuting the followers of Christ. Christ drastically changed Paul's value system. Paul became a man of compassion. God gave him the strength to endure personal torture so others might learn about Jesus, their Savior.

We want to pass on our values. It is part of our Christian heritage and witness, a God-given responsibility. Most of us take it seriously.

Since the beginning of the human family, God has expected parents to communicate His values to their children. After delivering the Ten Commandments to Moses, God commanded, "Impress them on your children. Talk about them when you sit at home and when you walk along the road, when you lie down and when you get up. Tie them as symbols on your hands and bind them on your foreheads. Write them on the doorframes of your houses and on your gates" (Deuteronomy 6:7–9).

In the New Testament, Paul comments on Timothy's sincere faith, "which first lived in your grandmother Lois and in your mother Eunice and, I am persuaded, now lives in you also" (2 Timothy 1:5).

My foremost prayer for my sons always has been that the Holy Spirit will keep their faith in Jesus as their Savior strong. Next in importance, I always have prayed that the Holy Spirit will help me pass on my values.

I often have claimed Proverbs 22:6, which tells me that if I train my children in the ways they should go, they will not depart from those ways when they were old. A close look at that verse gives a clue to the process of teaching children values. It doesn't say "tell" a child how to behave, it says "train a child." Training is based on "supervised practice." Think of how you train someone to drive a car, throw a ball, or learn any new skill. Training includes information in small increments (no long lectures) and an explanation of the goal and the standards for the behavior to be learned—followed by practice, review, evaluation, correction, practice, review, evaluation, more information, and so on. Training is an ongoing process with many steps.

Children are exposed to many different values. They receive conflicting and confusing messages about values because many adults in their lives do not share the same value system. Christian parents will want to help their children sort out the right messages from the wrong ones. Here are 10 steps to take as you share your value system with your children.

1. **Identify your own values.** Before you can teach your children, you need to be clear about what you want them to learn. Don't take a casual approach to this important parental responsibility. Take the time to develop a complete list of those qualities you plan to teach your children. This step includes asking God to direct and assist you in selecting the right values to teach your children.

2. **Tell your children what your values are**. Learn to state clearly and concisely what you believe and how these values influence decisions in your life. When telling your children about your values, paint word pictures, use analogies, and tell stories. Have your children tell you what you said to ensure that you have communicated clearly.

3. **Explain the values**. Telling children to be kind, loving, polite, generous, or patient does not give them sufficient information about what you expect. Instead, describe to your children the behaviors that demonstrate those qualities. Let your children know that when they behave in these ways, you are pleased with their choices. While you are not making your children responsible for your happiness, you do respond with pleasure when you see them doing right things because you are happy.

4. **Explore the values.** Help your children understand values by using a variety of teaching methods, inviting discussions about values, and allowing healthy debates. The more children understand individual values and how these are demonstrated in our lives, the more likely they are to adopt these values.

5. **Model what you want your children to say and do**. Your choices and commitment to values determines and shapes the kind of person *you are becoming.* You will want your children to observe you as a living model of the values you teach. Your children observe many people (teachers, friends, public figures, television characters, neighbors, family members) who may model conflicting values concerning goals, lifestyles, speech, morality, work, play, life, and death. Which models will they choose to follow? They may choose to follow your model or that of someone else or, more likely, choose different models to follow in different situations.

6. **Teach values with Bible stories**. Whenever you can teach a value by telling a Bible story, your children benefit twice. First, they learn more about values. Second, they also increase their knowledge and understanding of God's Word. Bible stories can come alive for children when they identify with the feelings and experiences of the characters. This is particularly true when they discover that the issues that confronted Jacob, Samson, David, and others—and the consequences of their choices—are much the same as those people face today.

7. **Apply values in everyday experiences.** The key to passing on values is to help children see how those values apply to daily life. Explain that choices reveal values. For example, a person who does a kind deed for a stranger demonstrates that kindness is one of his or her values. Look for and use teachable moments that provide an opportunity to choose between right and wrong, between good and bad. The situations may be real, on television, in a story you are reading, or something that happened in the past.

8. **Reinforce values through games**. Your children learn a lot about life as they play. Learning about values is not a boring, academic activity. Be creative and you will find many ways to make learning a game.

9. **Reward children when they live out Christian values**. We are quick to criticize and correct our children, but often we are slow with praise and rewards. Become a master of recognizing and rewarding your children when they do what you want them to do. Positive reinforcement effectively shapes children's choices.

10. **Celebrate as a family**. When your children pass a major milestone in their acceptance of the values you are teaching, make a big deal out of it. Don't just reward the choice, *celebrate*. This is what you have worked, prayed, and hoped would happen.

When you consistently take these 10 steps, you are doing all you can to teach your children the characteristics you value. You are doing your part. The rest is up to the Holy Spirit and your children. Each of us will make his or her own choices in life. There is no guarantee that your children will accept all the values you want them to adopt.

How Do Children Choose Values?

> *At an early age, Bill had been taught that stealing was wrong. He never took candy from the local grocery store, never stole a toy, never slipped money from his mom's purse. He didn't steal because he chose to be obedient. He followed what he had been told until he was 16. Then he and some friends stole a car and were arrested.*
>
> *While sitting in jail for a few hours, Bill evaluated his decision to help steal the car. He decided that he didn't like the consequences or the guilt he felt at being called a thief and that he would never steal again. And he didn't—not even a pencil from the office.*

Until he was 16, Bill followed his mother's value about stealing. However, through his experience, Bill accepted as a personal value that stealing was wrong. His experience reflects a four-step learning process.

1. **Understand the value**. Children cannot accept or adopt a value they do not understand. At first children may hear the words and think they know what their parents are trying to tell them, but children develop understanding over time as they hear, observe, and experience.

2. **Interact with the value**. Thinking is one aspect of developing values. The more we can stimulate our children to think, the better off they will be. Work to eliminate mindless behaviors and choices from

your children's lives. Teaching children to think well is a big task but a very important one. In Matthew 6:21, Jesus says what is stored in our hearts is what we are. What we think influences how we feel about an issue and how we act in a situation.

Encourage your children to interact with the value through explanations, explorations, applications, and discussions. Because feelings influence values, you will want to be aware of your children's emotional responses. All of us feel strongly about the values we hold most dear. When your children are angry, hurt, rejected, happy, excited, or validated, ask them to verbalize the value that has been rejected or affirmed by the experience. In this way you help them understand that beliefs influence emotional responses.

3. **Choose to accept a value as right**. When we set goals, we consider the options and consequences before choosing a course to pursue that goal. If we have a goal to improve our standard of living, we consider ways to get more money (take a second job, try for a promotion, change jobs or careers, inherit a million dollars, or win the sweepstakes, for example). After reviewing the possibilities, we may decide that a college degree would help us qualify for a promotion, so we enroll in classes. We know how to use the decision-making process.

Our children have to learn to make wise decisions. Sometimes they make choices with which we agree. At other times they make choices we believe to be wrong. While our children live at home, we often can control their behavior through discipline. However, being obedient to house rules does not mean that your children truly accept your values or that they personally have adopted them. We will only know a value has been accepted when our children are away from us, living on their own, and still making choices we believe to be right. Therefore, wise parents find ways to encourage children to make wise decisions about values.

> *When 14-year-old Lou said he wanted to become a mechanical engineer, his mom encouraged him to research the requirements, job market, average salary levels, and colleges. She found a mechanical engineer at church who spoke with Lou about her career. One night Lou and his mom discussed why engineering interested Lou; they listed other careers that might provide the same challenges. After a few weeks of active consideration, Lou was sure of his choice. He could have changed his mind as his values about the career were explored. But after truly exploring and making that choice, Lou was able to make subsequent decisions. Lou faithfully did his homework to keep his grades up so he could qualify for a college scholarship so he could become an engineer. Although the decision was his, part of Lou's eventual success as an engineer was a result of his mother, who took the time to help him make that personal choice.*

If we can encourage our children in making wise choices, they usually will turn away from inappropriate choices. Often, these choices are so diametrically opposed that one can't choose both. Matthew 6:24 outlines this principle: We cannot serve two masters. We cannot choose both God's way and the world's way. Thus, if we can lead our children in choosing well, we can shout with Joshua, "As for me and my household, we will serve the LORD!" (Joshua 24:15)

4. **Consistently demonstrate values by behavior**. As your children repeatedly and consistently act on their beliefs, their value system becomes an integral part of their lives. They become skilled in those actions and feel good about themselves in the process. When children tell you about a good choice they have made, identify the positive value they acted upon and affirm it.

> *Ten-year-old Mike shared his lunch with a classmate who had forgotten his. After school he proudly told the story. His mom responded, "Sounds like being a good friend is important to you."*
>
> *"Yeah, I like to be nice to my friends," Mike said, restating the value.*

Taking the right action is important. James 1:22–25 tells us that we must be doers, not just hearers, of the Word. And in James 4:17, God actually says that if we know what we should do and don't do it, we are sinning! Actions are critical, not only in our children's lives but also in our own.

Obstacles and Setbacks

There will be obstacles that hinder your efforts to teach values to your children.

• The values presented in many television shows and movies conflict with what you want your children to learn.

- Inappropriate role models can be seen as heroes. In some neighborhoods, for example, drug dealers are the ones with new cars, expensive clothes, jewelry, and money while a young child's hard-working father or mother may drive an old car, never have enough money, and wear inexpensive clothes. Without guidance in selecting values, the child who sees these two role models may choose to copy the drug dealer rather than the parent.

- Friends can be a problem if they influence your children to make choices based on values that conflict with yours. While you can limit the time spent with such friends, you will find it difficult to exclude them completely from your children's lives.

- Divorced parents often discover that the values at the other home are not the ones they embrace.

- Another obstacle may be us! If we fail to model the values we profess to be right, our actions speak louder than our words. Also, the way we present our values should not be preachy or nagging. We cannot expect our children to be carbon copies of us. They are unique persons, just as we are, and they will not necessarily be whom we wish them to become. In fact, aren't we all still becoming? I know I am still growing in many areas of my life.

However, if you use the 10 steps and the ideas in this book, you can overcome most of these obstacles. You can count on a few setbacks in the process of teaching your children values. Just when you think your children have accepted a value and you see them make God-pleasing choices, you may be surprised to see them behave in opposition to that value. Don't respond as if all were lost; it isn't. Consider this a temporary setback.

How often have you failed to live up to your personal values? Aren't there situations when you are tempted to make a choice you believe to be wrong? None of us is perfect. And re-deciding to adopt a value as part of their lives can be a reinforcing experience for your children.

So never give up hope. Never stop the teaching process. Never stop praying for your children. Never stop believing in them. Be the parent God created you to be. Never stop praying for His help. Teach your children Christian values.

Tips for Using This Book

Finding 501 ways to teach children values was quite a challenge! No one expects you to use every single idea in this book, and you will have many of your own creative ideas. Terrific! This book provides workable suggestions that you can use or modify to fit your situation.

Some activities are easy and require little planning or preparation. Others require a great deal of forethought and gathering of materials. Some are written specifically for young children, but you can adapt these into age-appropriate variations for older children. Some are written for older children and can be simplified for younger children. I have tried to give you activities geared to a variety of ages.

Many of the activities are well-suited to a single parent with one child, as well as to married parents with several children. When an activity requires more children than you have at home, either adapt the activity or include your children's friends.

I hope you will use this book as a reference for several years. As your children grow older, you can adapt the activities or use those written for older children. When an activity works well with your family, share that idea with a friend.

Remember Paul's exhortation to Timothy to continue passing on the faith his mother and grandmother had passed to him? When you share with others the things that seem to help your children adopt values based on God's Word, you are passing on hope, encouragement, and faith to others, just as Paul encouraged Timothy to pass the faith ... eventually to you and me. Now it is our turn to pass it on.

1 identify which values to teach

His face was red and wrinkled, his skin almost translucent, his hair virtually nonexistent. But to me he was the most beautiful baby in the world. As I watched my one-day-old son sleeping in my arms, I was overwhelmed with the enormity of the task of parenting this tiny person. "Oh, God! I don't feel smart enough. Please help me!" I prayed.

Just thinking of the many things I wanted to teach my son made me tired. How could I ever fit in all the lessons he would need to grow to be healthy, well-adjusted, mature, and to have a strong faith in God? Beyond learning to walk, feed himself, and talk, he would need to learn to drive a car, balance a checkbook, do the laundry, cook, clean, shop, relate with others, read, write, spell, discuss, analyze, prioritize, decide, work, and a thousand other things!

THERE ARE A LOT OF THINGS we can teach our children as they grow up: practical skills, safety practices, information about our world, historical facts, manners, art appreciation, music, conservation. The list is endless! But as parents the most important and awesome responsibility we have is to teach our children values. In Deuteronomy 6:7–9,

Moses told the Israelite parents that they were to take to heart the commandments of God and to impress these commandments upon their children. He said: "Talk about them when you sit at home and when you walk along the road, when you lie down and when you get up. Tie them as symbols on your hands and bind them on your foreheads. Write them on the doorframes of your houses and on your gates."

Moses emphasized that children learn values from ongoing instruction and discussion and from applying values to everyday experiences. Paul reminds us in Ephesians 6:4 to raise our children with "training and instruction of the Lord." We need the guidance of the Holy Spirit to teach our children values.

Which Values Will You Teach?

We constantly teach our children about our values. Some of that teaching is *unintentional.* As they listen and observe, our children learn what's important to us, what we consider right and wrong, what we believe, and what we expect from them. While we try to live according to what we believe is right, few of us manage to live up to our own standards all the time. When our actions match our words, our children get a consistent message. When our actions don't match our words, our children get confused.

That is why *intentional* teaching is so important. We can deliberately concentrate on values that we want our children to learn. The important first step in preparing to be an effective teacher is to identify and prioritize our personal values.

1. **Spend time in God's Word.** As you read, ask the Holy Spirit's guidance to identify your values and to develop a strategy for teaching them to your children. Repeatedly turn to God's Word, refresh yourself with His Meal, and continue to pray for guidance as you work through the successive steps.

2. **Make a comprehensive list of your values.** Limit the list to a reasonable number.

3. **Determine the best way to communicate these values to your children.** As your children grow, adjust your list and re-teach and reinforce your Christian values.

Here are some ideas to help you identify the values you will intentionally teach your children.

Read about teaching your children values. Make a comprehensive list of the different values these books suggest, then select the ones you want to emphasize. You may find the following books helpful: *Guiding Your Teen to a Faith That Lasts* by Kevin Huggins and Phil Landrum (Discovery House Publishers, 1994); *Teaching Your Child about God* by Wes Haystead (Regal Books, 1983); *Raising Ethical Children* by Steven C. Reuben (Prima Publishing, 1993); *Teaching Your Children Values* by Linda and Richard Eyre (Simon and Schuster, 1993); and *Fun Projects for Hands-On Character Building* by Rick and Marilyn Boyer (Homeschool Press, 1996).

List characteristics that are important to you. Ask yourself, "What characteristics do I look for in a friend?" or "How would I like to be remembered by my friends?" Brainstorm a long list, then identify your top priorities.

Read through the New Testament, especially the gospels, and list characteristics of Jesus. Read

Philippians 2:1–18 to refresh your thinking about the love that Jesus showed and to remind yourself that the Holy Spirit works in individuals to help us develop the "attitude of Christ."

Read about the attributes of God. God is: love (1 John 4:8); sovereign (Job 42:2); omnipotent (Job 38); omniscient (1 John 3:20); omnipresent (Psalm 139:7–13); holy (Leviticus 19:2) just (Deuteronomy 32:3–4); good (Nahum 1:7); wise (Romans 11:33); unchangeable (Malachi 3:6a); faithful (2 Timothy 2:13); everlasting (Isaiah 40:28); merciful (Psalm 116:5); and loving (John 3:16). Look up these attributes in a Bible dictionary to get a clearer picture of these characteristics of God. Then answer the question "What qualities do I want to develop in my life in response to these attributes of God?" Your response will begin the list of values that you will want to teach your children.

Read the Ten Commandments in Exodus 20:1–17. They are:

- Have no gods other than the one true God.
- Do not misuse the name of God.
- Keep the Sabbath holy.
- Honor your father and mother.
- Do not murder.
- Do not commit adultery.

- Do not steal.

- Do not give false testimony against another.

- Do not covet your neighbor's house.

- Do not covet your neighbor's spouse or property.

What qualities are suggested by these commandments? Make a list.

6 Read 2 Peter 1:1–11. Peter gives several qualities Christians are to develop in their lives. These include: faith, goodness, knowledge, self-control, perseverance, godliness, brotherly love. This is a good beginning list. What other qualities can you add to these?

7 Read 1 Corinthians 13. In this chapter, Paul describes *agape* love. He includes these characteristics: patient, kind, truth-loving, trusting, hopeful, protective, persevering, humble, meek, polite, unselfish, peaceable, and faithful. This passage suggests life characteristics that you will want to teach your children. Write them down.

8 Read Galatians 5:22–23 where Paul lists the fruit of the Holy Spirit in our lives: love, joy, peace, patience, kindness, goodness, faithfulness, gentleness, self-control. These are gifts the Holy Spirit gives as we mature in Christ. However, it is also possible to cultivate these qualities and to teach them to our children.

9 Read the biographies of several people you admire. Jot down the qualities in their lives that you value and appreciate. Consider which are the qualities you want to pass on to your children.

10 Write down all the values your parents attempted to teach you and your siblings. Then circle the ones you personally value. These are the values from your parents that you have "owned." You chose to accept these values. Notice those values you didn't accept. Ask yourself why you didn't agree with them. Was it because you received mixed messages from your parents about those qualities? Was it because you had a different perspective from your parents? Was it a rebellious act? Do you want to re-evaluate any values you have not accepted?

11 List people you consider to be heroes. What makes them admirable? Write down the qualities you value in each person. Are these values you would like your children to adopt?

12 Read Proverbs 31:10–31. Solomon describes a virtuous woman (which some scholars see as a personification of wisdom) in this passage. Many of the qualities are equally applicable to men. Some of the characteristics Solomon valued include: goodness, industry, creativity, provision, caring, negotiation, independence, strength, vigor, preparation, generosity, dignity, humor, wisdom, fear of God, enterprising, commitment, and sensitivity.

13

Write the obituary you would be honored to have written about you. Include the positive qualities you hope people will notice about you.

14

Read the following list and select the qualities you value: honesty, courage, peaceability, self-reliance, perseverance, self-discipline, moderation, fidelity, chastity, loyalty, dependability, respect, love, unselfishness, sensitivity, kindness, friendliness, justice, mercy, forgiveness, humility, self-confidence, risk-taking, faith in God, and gentleness.

15

Use a concordance to find Bible passages that address specific character qualities you want to teach to your children. Select the verses you will want to share with your children and encourage them to memorize these portions of Scripture. It is important that your children understand that what you are teaching them is scriptural. This is one way they can learn to apply the Bible to everyday life experiences.

16

Answer the following question: "What characteristics would the ideal person have?" After you make the list, rewrite it to be more realistic and practical. Use this second list to prioritize the values you will concentrate on teaching your children.

17

Read over your lists and eliminate the personality traits and skills. While you may find some personality traits to be more attractive than others and while you may value many different skills, you will want to focus on character traits for this exercise. Personality descriptions include: extrovert, introvert, analytical, creative, shy, focused, flexible, or intuitive.

18 Read about some of the godly persons described in Scripture. As you read, make a running list of the qualities that characterized these people. Which belong on your list for values to teach your children? Suggestions: Samuel, David, Elijah, Elisha, Hannah, Isaiah, Jonathan, Miriam, Mary (the mother of Jesus), Paul, Barnabas, Peter, Mary of Bethany, Lydia, and Dorcas.

19 Read the teachings of Jesus in the gospels, including the parables. What values did Jesus teach His disciples? Which are appropriate for you to teach your children?

20 Read the book of Galatians. List the characteristics Paul felt were important in the Christian life.

21 Read the book of Ephesians. List the characteristics Paul felt were important in the Christian life.

22   Read the book of Philippians. List the characteristics Paul felt were important in the Christian life.

23   Think of the different people in your family. What qualities in each person would you most like to teach your children?

24   Get together with two or three close friends. As a group, develop the list of qualities you each want to teach your children. Discuss the different values as you list them; it will help you prioritize the final list.

25   Ask your children what values they appreciate in others. List them all, then select the ones with which you agree. Add these to your list of values to teach. You can help them identify their values by asking: "What is important to you?" "Why is it important?" "When is it important?" "What would you do to get it?" "What would you not do to get it?" "What does this say about what you value?" "Do you find your values changing from situation to situation?"

2 communicate the values

Paula was running late for the evening meeting at church, but she took time to give last-minute instructions to her children, who were staying home with a sitter. "Remember, baths at 7:30 and bed at 8:30. Be nice to each other and no fighting."

Because they had heard these same instructions every time Paula left them with a sitter, the children nodded their heads and mouthed the instructions with Paula. She had effectively communicated this particular set of instructions. The children knew what Paula wanted them to do when she was gone.

ONCE YOU HAVE IDENTIFIED the values you intentionally will teach your children, you will want to effectively communicate these values to them. Remember Moses' instructions to parents. He said to talk with (notice it is "talk with" not "talk to") your children when you sit at home, when you walk along the road, when you lie down, and when you get up. He said to write the commandments of the Lord on the doorframes of the home and on the gates. (See Deuteronomy 6:6–9.) Telling children what you believe is right and what you want them to become is critical in the teaching process. Don't assume that because you are honest your children automatically will understand that honesty is something you value and want them to develop. Clearly communicate your top-priority values to your children. Telling children does not mean lecturing them *ad nauseam*. Instead, intentionally direct conversations so you can include comments about values as a natural part of the interaction. This way you are talking about your values in a way which children can understand and to which they can relate.

Effective communication involves more than sending a message. For real communication to occur, the message that is sent must be the same as the message received by the listener. So a part of communicating your values to your children involves verifying that what they heard is what you meant to say. One method of checking is to have your children repeat back what you said, using their own words. Listen closely to see if the message was distorted during transmission. Ask your children to give an example of how one could recognize that value in someone. Make sure they truly understand the behavioral outcome of adopting each value you teach them.

Remember that just telling children something in no way ensures that they will accept the value as true for them. If *telling* worked perfectly, we would all be perfect because we have been *told* how to behave by our teachers, preachers, parents, neighbors, friends, authors, and dozens of other people!

Recognize that even if children do what you tell them (such as being truthful, helpful, kind, or courteous) they may not have accepted your values as their own. They simply may be acting obediently to please you or to avoid punishment. The test of acceptance is when children choose to act in accordance with those values when you aren't around or when there are no parental consequences for not doing so.

When children are very young, you can be direct when instructing them about values. You can tell them what to do, what is right, what is wrong, what is good, and what is unacceptable. However, as they grow older, children will respond better if you progress from ordering to persuading and advising. Parents who remain in the "ordering" phase often find at some point that children rebel against the authoritarian approach. Communicating values is an action the parent takes. Accepting values and owning them is an action the child takes. Telling children about values is only the first step in passing on these values.

Here are some ways to communicate your values to your children using written, recorded, or spoken words.

Clearly tell your children what you expect them to become in terms of values. If you want them to become caring, loving people, you might say, "You are going to grow up to be a very loving person. You can start now by showing people how much you love them." Then list several ways your children can demonstrate love.

If you were emphasizing truthfulness, you might say, "I expect you to always tell the truth. Sometimes it will be hard, but I want you to be an honest person. I want to be able to believe you whenever you tell me something." Frequently include such statements in your talks with your young children to impress these expectations upon them. Even with older children, you cannot rely on a casual mention to suffice. Communicating your values is an ongoing process. As your children grow and develop a greater ability to understand your values, the way you tell them about these values changes. You can give more information, additional explanations, and the reasons why these values are important in life.

27 Frequently share what you value and why. This differs from telling your children what you expect of them. With this method, you attach significance to the values and also show that these values apply to your life. Say things such as "I value honesty." "I love truth-telling." "I think it is very important to tell the truth because ..." The way you complete that sentence must make sense to your child if you hope to transfer the value.

You can set the stage so your children's choices correspond to your values. Before you ask, "Who ate the plate of cookies I had on the table?" first say, "I appreciate honesty." Or say, "It pleases me when you tell the truth, especially when you don't want to do so." Or say, "Sometimes it is hard to tell the truth, but when you are honest, you make me happy." In these cases, remember to consider what is more important, teaching values or punishing whoever ate the cookies you made for a neighbor. From the eternal perspective, it is better to help your children learn to tell the truth than to punish them for spoiling your kind gesture. (On the other hand, if you had given specific instructions not to eat the cookies, you may have additional considerations that will influence your response.)

28 Write out the values you want to characterize your family members. The language and length of what you write needs to be consistent with the age and comprehension level of each child. Read what you have written to your children. Then post it on the refrigerator, family bulletin board, or another location. At least once a week, read part or all the description to your children. When they are old enough to read, allow your children to take turns reading the values for the family.

Although you will want to teach your children many values, your list should be those top-priority values or those you currently are emphasizing with your children.

29 Take time to find Bible verses that advocate the values you are teaching your children. Read these as part of family devotions or during a special time when you focus on values. Read the verses in several Bible versions so you can find the best version to use with your children. While you may claim the King James Version as your favorite, other contemporary language versions are easier for children to understand.

30 Work as a family to make banners to hang in the family room, one for each major value you want to emphasize. The banners may be felt or cloth with embroidery or appliqués; strips of shelf paper that you color or paint; or computer printouts you designed. Even if your children are very young, find ways to include them in the process of creating the banners. While you can make the banners yourself, the process of working together is helpful. As you work, you can talk about the value you are depicting. You can discuss the value and give examples of that value in behavioral terms. You don't have to make all the banners at once; you can spend several weeks on this project.

You won't want to display a banner for more than a week at a time. Studies of the effectiveness of posters and signs in the workplace have proven that once people get used to seeing a particular poster or sign, they stop reading it. That's why many companies change safety posters weekly. Take a lesson from industry and increase the effectiveness of banners as a teaching medium.

31 Make posters that illustrate your values. Posters are similar to banners, but smaller. Posters can be illustrated with a variety of things: pictures from magazines, drawings, photographs from your family album, lettered words, words or letters cut from newspapers or magazines, or items that are glued down (cloth cutouts, beans, macaroni, seeds, craft sticks, buttons, etc.). There are no limits to how creative you can be when making posters.

Your family may make several different posters, one for each of your top values. You also may make one or more posters that include all the top values. The family may work together on the posters or each family member can make his or her own. Post them for a week at a time to communicate your values to your children and to guests.

32 Collect quotations (from speakers, *Reader's Digest,* books you read, or any other source) that comment on or clearly state one of the values you want your children to adopt. Share these with your children during a family time, over dinner, or as part of a one-on-one conversation. Copy the quotations and post them on the refrigerator, family bulletin board, or another location. Replace them from time to time, but save the old ones for re-posting at a later date.

Start a notebook with a different page for each value and the relevant quotations written underneath. This notebook will be a good resource when you use other teaching methods.

33 Write individual letters to your children telling them what you want them to become and the values you want them to adopt and why. As your children grow older, you will want to write new letters to them to expand on the basic expectation.

Jason wrote his 8-year-old daughter the following letter.

Dear Tiffany,

I love you. I am proud of you. As your dad, I plan to teach you to become all the things God wants you to be. Some of these things are: an honest girl who always tells the truth so people know they can trust your word; a loving girl whose friends know you really care about them; a good student who does her best; and a girl who loves God.

When I see you doing these things, I feel happy, and I promise to let you know how much I appreciate these things in you. I pray for you every day that God will help you grow into a terrific young woman.

Your loving dad

34 Surprisingly, many children's books intentionally communicate values. It will not be difficult to find children's books that give examples of many values you want to teach. Read these books aloud to your children, beginning when they are young. Later, they can take turns reading the stories to the family. It is important that you be a part of the story reading and listening. Sometimes you may have one child read to another, but don't do this all the time.

35 Spend time "painting the picture" of how your children can be in the future. Say, "How I see you when you are all grown up is …"

Eleanor is very good at this. She told Kyle, her 10-year-old son (who was interested in computer games): "I can see you working in a company that makes computer games. You test new games to be sure they work. People who design games get excited when they learn you will be testing their games because you are good at discovering things that make the game better. You work hard. Your boss knows that you are dependable and don't have to be watched all the time. Your boss also knows that your reports on computer games are accurate because you always tell the truth. If you say you tested a game, then you did. If you say that a problem has been corrected in a game, then it has been. Your boss is happy with you because you are honest, hard-working, and dependable. You even get raises every year because of the good job you do."

Because Eleanor frequently painted this picture for her son—sometimes emphasizing other values, sometimes describing the office space he might work in, sometimes describing his relationships with friends—Kyle came to like and believe in the reality. Even before he left high school, he was in touch with a computer game company and had a promise of a job after graduation. Part of Kyle's success was a result of a mother who could paint an effective word picture.

Word pictures need to be descriptive, include emotions (notice how Eleanor said that game designers got "excited" and that his boss "was happy"), and be attractive to the child.

Use different occasions to discuss values with your children. As Moses said, talk whenever you are together. You can initiate informal discussions in the family room, at bedtime (children love an excuse to delay going to sleep), or while working on chores or a project. Many parents find that children respond more candidly when discussions are informal and when the parent is actively engaged in doing something besides talking. Examples include washing dishes together or driving in the car. Children often clam up when a parent asks questions or talks with them face to face.

> *Shelly shares: "When I want to have a serious discussion with one of my children, I invite him or her to go to the store with me. We have great conversations in the car, pushing a shopping cart along the store aisles, or standing in line at the post office. If necessary, I'll even invent errands if I need to talk with one of the kids."*

However, there also is nothing wrong with having face-to-face discussions about values. Just be sensitive to how your children respond and plan discussions accordingly.

37

Take older children to professional lectures and seminars that emphasize the values you are teaching. These might be hosted by a local Bible college, church, Christian organization, or city-wide youth ministry.

Make the event special by going out to lunch or dinner before or after the lecture. Select a place that would be a special treat for your child. Take good notes at the lecture so you can refer back to what was said in later discussions about values. Such references tend to underscore the importance of the lecture and to prolong the positive effects.

38

For older children, purchase motivational audiocassettes or videocassettes that emphasize values with which you agree. Inquire at a Christian bookstore about what is available. The store often will have catalogs you can scan. Check with your pastor, youth worker, women's group coordinator, or men's group coordinator in your church for leads. Other good sources for these tapes are Christian radio programs.

39

Make your own recording about your values. You can build your own audio (or video) library for your children. Write a script, be sure it says everything you want it to, then record it. Hearing your voice on the recording is a nice touch, especially for young children. You can play the recordings for your children as they go to sleep or at other appropriate times. Keep them short enough to hold attention— five to seven minutes. Make several "programs" to cover the topic but keep each program short and to the point.

40 Stencil curtains that illustrate your values. You may not actually write your values on the doorframes of your home (as Moses suggested), but there are many ways you can illustrate or list your values throughout your home. Making curtains is just one option. You could do the same with covers for throw pillows, pictures for the walls, murals painted on the walls, bedspreads, clothing appliqués, schoolbook covers, etc.

Do several of these things, but don't do them all at once. Do one or two a month for maximum effectiveness. Let your children become used to one new way of telling them about your values. When they no longer notice that one, add another one.

41 Bake fortune cookies with your own messages about values inside. As a family member eats a cookie, he or she reads the message to the rest of the family and explains how that message works in real life. Make this a project for a gloomy day. Involve your children in writing the messages, making the dough, inserting the messages, and baking the cookies. Make lots. Serve the cookies at dinner once a week or twice a month until you run out. Sample messages include: "Friends love one another." "Loving is doing." "Be honest no matter what the situation." "Success comes from hard work." "Kind deeds make new friends."

42 After watching a television show or movie together, give your thoughts about how the characters' actions reflect values. Children tend to get caught up in the story without identifying the values portrayed. However, parents can use this opportunity to point out the values they want to emphasize. This method also helps children learn to step back from situations and look for the values.

"I wouldn't want Shane for my best friend," Gary commented to his son after watching a situation comedy together. *"He didn't tell the truth about what happened at school. He was very selfish with his bike. And he would rather cheat on a test than study and learn the information for himself."*

Duane nodded in agreement. "He was funny, though, Dad," he added.

"Yes, he was funny, but for me that wouldn't make up for the negative qualities," Gary responded.

Duane thought for a minute, then said, "I think that Eddy was a better friend. He told the truth, and he was kind to the new guy at school."

Gary agreed. "Being a good friend and a kind person is very important. When people are kind to me, I feel happy and loved," he said, including an emotional tie-in to the value.

Write your top-priority values on index cards. On the back of each card, write a brief definition of the value. You can use the cards in different ways. Your children can try to define the values and compare their definitions to the ones you have written. Your children can read the definitions you have written and guess which value is being described. Or you can simply read one of the cards (front and back) before dinner. If you do this, you might read the same value card every night for two weeks. This helps your children learn the definition through repetition. You might even read the definition and have your children repeat it after you each night. If the definition is long, read it in phrases and have them repeat the phrases after you.

With your children, make quilts that list and illustrate the values you want them to learn. Alternate patterned squares with white squares embroidered with the values. (You can use either liquid or thread embroidery.)

If your child is interested in animals, use coloring book outlines of animals that represent the value on each quilt square, for example: a lion for courage, a kitten for gentleness, a dove for peacefulness, an ant for industry (Proverbs 6:6–8), or a dog for loyalty. When the quilt cover is finished, add batting and a back. You can quilt it on the sewing machine, by hand, or simply tie it with crochet thread at the corners of each square.

Have mugs made for your children with your values written on them. Use your computer to type out the values using different fonts or print the values in different colors. You can design individual mugs for each child with his or her photo and a description that includes the values you want to teach. Hint: Rather than writing "Sally *is* an honest, caring, kind, loyal, dependable, self-disciplined young woman," use "*is becoming.*" This is a more appropriate description of all of us. None of us has arrived at his or her personal development goals in all areas of values, but we are all *becoming* what Christ is leading us to be.

Use the mugs once a week for a special treat: soup broth, cocoa before bed, hot cider, orange-cinnamon tea, or some other drink your children enjoy.

46 Together, make signs, pictures, or plaques for your children's rooms that list values. Enlarge a favorite photograph and write on it with white, gold, or silver ink before framing it. Plaques are easy to make from a picture or lettered sign, a small piece of wood (5″ × 7″), and a hook for hanging. A coat of varnish over the plaque gives it a nice finish. Signs can be of all varieties. Road signs, street signs, or directional signs are unique and colorful and can be adapted for values decorations.

47 Order several sets of pencils from a mail order house. Instead of printing your children's names on the pencils, print values. Or use a phrase such as: "The Butler family values honesty." "The Smith family values dependability." "The Jones family values self-discipline." Give each child one pencil from each set. Or give the children the pencils one at a time, depending on which value you currently are emphasizing as a family.

48 Make a tablecloth for informal family dinners. It could be vinyl, plastic, or cloth. It might be fun to use plain material as a tablecloth for one dinner. When the dishes have been cleared off, invite the family to be creative with tubes of liquid embroidery paint or permanent markers. You can write or draw, but somewhere on the tablecloth each of your top-priority values should be listed.

49 Cross-stitch an old-fashioned sampler that states your values. Design a different sampler for each child who is old enough to cross-stitch his or her own. Children can give these as presents, hang them in their rooms, group them on a family values wall, or rotate the different samplers in the family room.

50 Have a classroom-style values training session for your children. Tailor the length of the session to the age and attention span of your children. Use lecture as part of the session, but use creative methods (from the different chapters in this book) for the remainder.

explain the values

"Then I found out that Kerry lied," 8-year-old Melanie told her mother. "Tammy never said I was ugly!"

"I can take almost anything except being lied to," Gwen said with emphasis. "I hate it when I find out I've been deceived. I feel betrayed and have a hard time ever trusting that person again." Then Gwen asked Melanie how she felt when she discovered that a friend had lied to her.

"I felt angry." Melanie admitted.

"Tell me about another time someone lied to you and you felt angry." Gwen invited.

As Melanie remembered the experience and told the story to her mom, she spoke with strong feelings left over from the incident. Gwen listened and indicated that she knew how Melanie felt. Gwen then asked Melanie to think of how her friend could have been honest.

Gwen wasn't surprised when Melanie looked up and said with determination, "I tell the truth. I'm never going to lie!"

MELANIE'S PROMISE WAS SINCERE, but she would need to experience many situations in which she would be tempted to lie—and to act on her resolve to be honest—before that value would be truly her own. However, her decision that day was a great beginning.

Gwen's next step in teaching Melanie would be to explain honesty so Melanie could understand all that being honest means. Gwen also would have to explore the different ways to be honest or dishonest. Just telling Melanie to be honest isn't enough for her to learn honesty.

There are many ways to explain values to children and to help them understand. These methods don't require that you do all the talking, just that you guide the learning process so your children can picture your priority values for themselves. Part of the picture is knowing which behaviors demonstrate the value and which demonstrate the opposite. When explaining honesty to Melanie, Gwen will talk about whether pretending to like something you don't like is honest or dishonest. She will talk about doing one's own homework as honest and cheating on a test as dishonest, outright lying as dishonest, as well as keeping quiet and letting someone else be blamed for one's actions as dishonest. She will help Melanie see that honesty is keeping her word and doing what she says she will do.

Just as it is for Gwen, one of your jobs as a parent is to explain your values in behavioral terms. Help your children recognize the emotional results of behaving in accordance with each value. In other words, it feels good to do the right thing. While feelings are not the basis for making God-pleasing decisions, it is true that wise decisions make us feel good inside. And our actions affect the feelings of friends and parents. Help your children learn to recognize that making wise decisions helps them feel good about themselves. Even if there is a negative consequence (for example, loss of popularity with friends when one refuses to go along with wrong decisions), there is inner knowledge that one has pleased God and chosen to do what is right.

Share with your children the Scripture passages that tell how God loves children (even when they make mistakes) and especially delights in them when they do what is right. Psalm 1 is one example where a person delights in following God's law and the Lord prospers him. Remind your children often that Jesus faced every temptation and decision we face and stands ready to help us with every choice.

Your goal is to help your children develop a positive emotional response to adopting each of your values. When your child comes home from school and proudly tells you how well he or she did on a spelling or history test, express your positive response, then affirm your child's positive response. Say, "When you work hard and do well, you feel proud, don't you?" Then ask, "What else do you feel?" Encourage children to identify as many positive feelings that come from acting on one of the values you have been teaching. Encourage them to bask in those positive feelings. During supper, invite them to share what they did and how good it made them feel. Express your positive thoughts so the entire family can understand how you respond to positive behaviors and choices.

Let your children know how pleased, happy, excited, thrilled, joyous, satisfied, and proud you are when they demonstrate your values. And you also may let them know how disappointed, displeased, unhappy, depressed, sad, upset, angry, and embarrassed you are when they act on values that are opposite from yours. The focus of the emotional response must be the behavior, not the child. Don't say, "I am unhappy when you are a bad boy." (Notice the message is "you are a bad boy." Instead say, "Even though I love you, when you are unkind, I feel very disappointed." This way it becomes more clear to your child that you are rejecting the behavior, not the child. It is important to explain why you feel disappointed, angry, or sad. If your explanation makes sense to your child, it will have greater impact on the future. Give the positive feedback both individually to your child and in front of the rest of the family, but only give negative feedback individually. A good rule is "Praise in public; correct in private."

A third aspect of explaining emotional response to behavior is helping your children know that other people will respond emotionally to what they do and how they behave. The primary responder will be the person who is directly affected by the behavior: the friend who is treated unkindly, the schoolmate with whom your child is unselfish, the friend who discovers your child to be loyal, and the child at school who is positively impacted by your child's self-control. In explaining these responses to your children, it is most effective to have them describe how they respond to the actions of others. Once they have identified these feelings (just as Melanie did), they can better understand how others will respond to their actions.

The secondary responder is the person who observes your children's actions but isn't directly affected by them. This category of responders includes teachers, pastors, other adults, and even other children who come to know your child by his or her actions. As children recognize that there are many consequences for their actions, they develop a greater understanding of the importance of the values you are teaching them.

Here are some ways to explain values to your children and to help them understand the meaning of these values.

51 Share stories from your personal experiences to illustrate how you made choices consistent with your values. As you tell each story, describe the choice you faced, the decision you made, how you felt, the outcome of your decision, and the way others responded. Your teaching stories might include:

sticking up for a friend, not going along with a group that was planning to do something against your convictions, times when you were kind to a stranger, or an incident when it took courage to make the right choice.

With older children, consider sharing the occasional story from your past when you did not make the wise choice and suffered the consequences. This probably is not the best teaching option for younger children, but it can be powerful with older teenagers. Examples might include when you stayed out past your curfew and had to miss a special event because you were grounded, or a time when you told a half-truth and were not only embarrassed but lost credibility with a friend.

52

Make your children aware of some of your inner struggles. Instead of fussing and fuming when another driver cuts in front of you, release your feelings by sharing them with your children. Make sure you don't yell at the driver, make inappropriate gestures, or use your car to gain advantage over the other driver. Instead, verbalize your anger. Say with feeling: "When someone does what that driver just did, I immediately become angry." Admit your temptation: "What I want to do is yell, shake my fist, and pull ahead of the other car." Acknowledge your choice: "But I know that doing those things is not a good witness as a Christian. Even though I really want to act out my anger, I will choose not to do so."

Act on your choice. Slow down if necessary and wave the other driver into the lane. Smile. Then explain your feelings about doing the right thing:

"When I make the right decision and act kindly toward someone, I feel better inside. I know that God approves of what I just did. That makes me happy. It doesn't matter if the other driver is kind. I chose to be a kind person, and I will act on that value."

53 Explain your personal response to the values shown by other people in real-life situations, on television, in movies, or in stories. If you notice one of your children working for a long time to repair a bicycle or solve a computer game, take time to point out that he or she is demonstrating patience or perseverance. Say that you are impressed. (Remember that your child may not have thought about values while working on the project. He or she may not even be aware that values are involved in the activity.) Acknowledge that it often is frustrating to keep working at something when you can't seem to see progress. Affirm these qualities in your child and explain that this behavior is a good example of the values you want in the family. Describe the good feelings you have when you notice your children acting in accordance of your values. Don't forget to reward the behavior.

54 When you read Bible stories with your children, ask them how the different characters demonstrated a particular value. (Name one of the values you are stressing at that time.) For example, when reading the story of David and Mephibosheth (2 Samuel 9:1–13), you might ask how King David demonstrated kindness, friendship, or generosity. You might ask how Mephibosheth demonstrated courage or respect.

Note: You will get better answers to questions such as these if you ask the questions before you read the story. That way your child will know what to listen for. Keep this in mind for any activities where you want children to listen for specific information.

55 When you read a newspaper story that illustrates one of your values, clip it out and share it with your children. (If you watch a particularly good story on the television evening news, you could use it.) Look for stories that help explain values such as courage, kindness, loyalty, caring, honesty, faithfulness, self-discipline, or perseverance. Hint: You can find great stories in *Reader's Digest* and *Guideposts*.

Discuss what behaviors in the story communicate values to you. Explain your response to those behaviors. Ask, "How do you feel when you hear about people acting this way?" When your children have shared, say something such as, "When I read about people acting in this way, I get excited because I know they had difficult choices to make and it took courage to make the right one." (Children are much more interested in hearing your response *after* you have listened to theirs.)

56 When you notice your values demonstrated by other people, point this out to your children. If you're at the mall and notice a boy who helps a woman pick up her packages, point this out. (Or tell your children about it if they weren't with you.)

Identify the behavior with a value. Say, "The boy was helpful (or kind) because he noticed the woman needed help and he stopped to help her. He didn't appear to have any personal motive; he just responded to someone's need. I admire that boy. When I see someone being kind, I feel warm inside and pleased. I imagine that the woman also felt happy when the boy helped her. And I am sure the boy also felt good about himself. Isn't it great how being kind can make so many people feel good?"

57 Find fables that make moral points consistent with your values and read them to your children. Many of the fairy tales and fables from the past help explain important values while entertaining children. After reading the fable or fairy tale, encourage your children to draw pictures that illustrate the story and the values suggested by the characters' actions. Post the art projects on the refrigerator or the family bulletin board for a week.

58 Set aside an evening to play charades. On slips of paper, write brief descriptions of someone acting out one of your top-priority values. Fold up the papers and put them in a shoe box. Each family member takes turns drawing one and using charades to communicate the value. The other family members take turns guessing the value. The family member who best communicates values through the charades gets to select the evening treat for the family. Decide ahead of time how you will determine who will win. It could be the person who correctly guesses the most values or whose charades were easiest to guess. Here are some examples.

- **Kindness**—A boy shares his lunch with a friend.

- **Loyalty**—A friend stands by someone who isn't popular with the other kids.

- **Honesty**—A girl breaks a cup and tells the truth when her mother asks who did it.

- **Self-discipline**—A child becomes angry but restrains the angry response and stays calm.

- **Patience**—A person waits in line patiently, even if the salesperson is very slow.

If you have young children (ages 4 to 7), work through the short, interactive devotions in *A Family Garden of Christian Virtues* by Susan Lawrence (Concordia, 1997). If your children are a little older (ages 6 to 10), read the stories in *Ways to Grow: 101 Virtue-Building Devotions* by Eldon Weisheit (Concordia, 1997). As you read the stories, discuss the decisions the characters make. Ask how their faith in Jesus guided their thinking. Tell about similar experiences from your own life and encourage your children to share as well. Other good resources are *The Family Book of Christian Values* by Stuart and Jill Briscoe (Chariot Family Publishing, 1995) and *The Children's Book of Virtues* by William J. Bennett (Simon and Schuster, 1995).

As a family, write definitions for your top-priority values. The process of writing definitions helps clarify one's understanding of the values. You can collaborate on a definition or you each can write your own definition and share what you have written with the others. Then write a definition that draws from all your definitions. While we may think we know what a specific value means, we still have difficulty writing clear definitions. After you have agreed on a definition, refer to the dictionary and see how that definition is similar to, and different from, the one you have written. Display the definitions somewhere in your home.

61

Tell your children a story, fairy tale, or fable that emphasizes one of your values and help them write (or record) a parallel story in a contemporary setting with children of their own age. This process leads children to apply the principles to their lives. Instead of just hearing a nice story, your children can identify with the characters, decisions, and values. Be sure to include the results of making wise decisions. Whenever possible, include in the story the spiritual implications of the value. Close the story with "And God was very pleased that _____ (name the main character) decided to be _____ (name the value illustrated by the story)."

62

Use the role reversal technique as a teaching tool. Ask your children to roleplay parents while you play a child. Their task is to teach you about a value. Choose a specific value for them to teach. They probably will start by simply telling you to be whatever that value is. As you know, telling is important but not enough. In your role as the learner, ask questions so your children are challenged to find new ways to explain the value to you.

If you have assigned your children the task of teaching you to be patient, ask: "What does it mean to be patient?" "Why do I have to be patient?" "What does it look like when a person is being patient?" "If I don't feel like being patient, how can I act patiently?" "What if people take advantage of my patience?" "What is the benefit of being patient?" "Why would God want me to be patient?"

Have fun with the roleplay. Use silly examples or make ridiculous comments so your children laugh. Keep the mood light and positive. Phrase your questions carefully so you don't frustrate your children into giving up. As your children answer your questions, they will increase their personal understanding of the value.

Leaf through magazines and note the different advertisements. Challenge your children to identify what value the advertisers are "selling." Many advertisements are designed to lead people to believe that using or owning a particular product will make them sexy, irresistible, popular, enviable, and successful. Other advertisements make claims that their product is better than all the competitors, which may or may not be true. When you have identified the value the advertisement is selling, work together to redesign the advertisement (if possible) to sell a value that you agree is important. For example, a perfume advertisement might sell the idea of irresistible sexuality and desirability. A redesigned advertisement for the perfume might sell the idea of being pleasant to be around and show parents surrounded by children in a "group hug." The headline might read "Love the scent that reminds you of home." As you can see, even this example could be interpreted as giving the wrong message (use this perfume and you will have a loving family). Writing advertisements that would reflect your top-priority values is not easy. But the process of trying allows your children to wrestle with understanding those values and, therefore, can be a great learning experience.

64 Reflect back to when you first owned each of your top-priority values. What experience brought you to a point where you chose that specific value as part of who you are? What led to your decision? Before that, had you acted on that value because of obedience to your parents or God? When did you first become aware of that value? Who told you about it?

When you can clearly identify the first time you chose a value for yourself, think of subsequent incidents when you acted on your choice. What helped you remain committed to that value? What helped you resist temptation to act opposite of that value? Can you think of times when God provided divine intervention to help you make the right choice? (For example, were you tempted to lie in a certain situation, but, just as you were about to speak, someone interrupted and sidetracked the conversation?) Share these things with your children.

65 Work as a family to write acrostics using the names of your top-priority values. The acrostic should help define the value. Here's an example.

H	=	Honorable
O	=	Open
N	=	Noble
E	=	Equitable
S	=	Straightforward
T	=	Truthful
Y	=	"Yes" means "yes"

You can use phrases if you can't come up with exact words. And if certain letters seem impossible to use in the acrostic format, make an exception and use a word that has that letter in it. For example, the "y" in the *honesty* acrostic could stand for *veracitY*.

Have fun with this assignment. Don't let it become frustrating. If you can't make an acrostic with some values, put them aside and work on others. Perhaps you will think of new words at a later time. It is best to wrestle with ideas and think of words on your own. Use a dictionary or a thesaurus, but only refer to them when you are truly stumped. Also keep adult input to a minimum. The goal is to have your children increase their understanding of the values. This means the more you "tell" them, the less they will learn from this activity.

Using sheets of construction paper for the background, design word pictures for each value. Write the value in the center of the paper. Then cut out words and phrases from newspapers and magazines that relate to the value or illustrate it. Glue or tape these words to the construction paper in a random arrangement or in a shape (circle, triangle, square) around the value. Older children may use the cutout words to make a design, a figure outline, or to illustrate the value in some other way. Display the values word pictures one at a time, rotating them at least once a week.

67 Use index cards to develop situation flash cards that involve your top-priority values. Make at least five cards for each value. Write the name of the value at the top of the card. Then have your children help you think of situations that involve the value. Write a brief description of the situation, then write a "what if" question about what would happen if the value were followed in that situation. An example for a card on self-control might be:

> *You are walking to school and a kid speeds by you on her bicycle. Just as she passes you, the bicycle runs through a mud puddle and splashes you. The kid just keeps going and doesn't stop. If you were to exercise self-control, what would you do?*

Another way to approach writing the situations is to ask your children, "When would a person need to exercise self-control?"

Developing the cards will help your children understand more about how values are involved in everyday situations. At another time you can use the cards as discussion starters. Select a card at random, give it to one child to read and answer. Then the card is passed to the next child who responds using a different answer or example. Continue until each family member has responded to the question. This will help your children recognize that there are many ways to demonstrate the value by their behavior.

68 On the way home from church ask your children to identify the values that tie into the day's sermon. (Hint: Both you and your children will want to listen to the sermon with this assignment in mind so you can identify related values.)

69 As a family, start a notebook of values. Include stories about how each of you felt when a specific value was demonstrated. Use quotations, photographs of incidents when you or your children acted in accordance with your values, and anything else to help paint a clearer picture of how the value might look in real life. Keep this notebook with other family projects such as definitions, posters, signs, newspaper clippings, or achievement charts for different values.

70 Think about each of your top-priority values. Then brainstorm with your children a list of ways to demonstrate each value. Try to come up with at least 25 different behaviors for each value. The first ideas will be the most familiar, but as the list increases, your children will have to do some serious thinking about how behaviors indicate values. If your children easily list 25 behaviors for a specific value (such as love), then invite them to set a higher number as the goal for that value. Say, "How many more ways do you think you can come up with? That's exciting. Let's try it."

Discuss the lists you have developed. Talk about which behaviors are easy and which take genuine commitment to the value. Share experiences where each of you have demonstrated your values by your behaviors.

71

If your family is on the Internet, spend an evening evaluating websites and determining which (if any) values are illustrated on-line. An excellent place to begin is www.gospelcom.net. From that home page you can access almost 100 Christian websites. Two websites your children would enjoy are The Children's Bible Hour at www.gospelcom.net/cbh and The Children's Sonshine Network at www.gospelcom.net/csn. By downloading the free RealAudio player (from www.realaudio.com), your children can listen to recorded programs.

The ministries that have websites on the Gospel Communications Network have different priorities and objectives for those websites, but the values behind them are those with which you should agree, even if they are not on your top-priority list.

Afterward, you might design your own values website with a different page for each value. The home page could have a brief description of values and their importance. Then you could list your top-priority values and "link" them to the individual value pages. If you have software to design an actual website, this could become an exciting project. If you don't have the necessary software (or a computer), make a "paper" website using individual sheets of paper for each page.

72

Spend an evening writing letters to newspaper and magazine editors that express your approval or disapproval of the values illustrated in their publications.

Think of rituals or traditions you can develop for your family to demonstrate your values. You could set aside the first Saturday morning of each quarter to show kindness to others. During the next 12 weeks you can discuss what to do and for whom in preparation for the next quarter's project. Or you could teach your children how to give a warm, firm handshake and decide that it will be your family ritual to greet people with a welcoming handshake.

Write statements about each of your top-priority values to use for an agree/disagree exercise. If you include phrases such as "the most important" or "the most essential," your statements become subject to debate. This is your goal. For example, write, "The most important thing about honesty is always telling the whole truth." Obviously, you can agree with parts of this statement and disagree with part of it. As your children state why they agree or disagree, they will learn more about the value.

Develop a quiz on values. Give a prize for the child who scores the highest, but take into consideration the age of each child, especially if there is more than four years between your oldest and youngest.

Develop a self-evaluation form that lists your top-priority values. Ask family members to rate themselves from one to 10 for each value. A rating of one indicates that the person hasn't learned or practiced that value. A rating of 10 indicates that the person practices that value all the time. Encourage honesty in the ratings by saying the ratings will not be shared. In general terms, discuss values you each need to integrate better into your lives.

77 Spend an evening encouraging your children to tell what they have learned about values and what experiences have helped them learn.

78 Encourage your children to develop a personal conscience. One way is to have them consider the following question before making important choices: "When I look back at this situation, how will I feel about the choice I made, and what will I think of myself?

79 On a sheet of paper, list your values in a column on the left side. In a column on the right side, list the opposites of your values. Cut up the lists and put the slips of paper in a bowl. Family members can take turns drawing a slip of paper, reading it, then stating whether the concept is helpful or hurtful and why. After all the slips of paper have been read, have your children match your values with their opposites.

80 Discuss your top-priority values and identify the obstacles we encounter when we act on each value. As each obstacle is identified, talk about ways to overcome it.

81 Have your children make personalized nameplates for their bedroom doors. The nameplates would include their photographs, their names, and a list of the values each child has demonstrated in the last several months.

82

Make collages with magazine pictures, phrases, and words to illustrate one of your top-priority values. After the collages are completed, have each person describe and explain his or her collage.

83

Make a montage that illustrates values. Begin with a small box approximately one-foot square. Turn it upside down and decorate each of the four sides and the top to illustrate different values. You could use magazine pictures, words, and phrases, or your own drawings. When the montage is finished, have each family member explain what he or she added to the project and how it illustrates values.

84

Using a large sheet of flip chart paper, make a composite drawing of one of your top-priority values. Draw a scene in which someone is practicing the value. Younger children can add grass, trees, and flowers. Older children can draw people. Everyone participates in planning the picture.

85

Develop family mottoes for each of your top-priority values. These mottoes can be added to your family values scrapbook, posted on the refrigerator, or displayed in some other way.

86 Have your children collect job announcements or employment applications from a variety of employers. Also clip out help-wanted advertisements from the newspaper. See if your children can determine from the application forms, job announcements, or advertisements what values employers seek in applicants. Discuss how these values are similar to or different from those you emphasize for your family.

87 Have your children interview or survey employers to learn what values they are looking for in applicants. Discuss how these values are similar or different from your values. Talk about how one becomes the kind of person an employer would want to hire.

88 Have your children do a character analysis of a person found in the Bible, a character on a television show, or an historical character. Which of your values did the person demonstrate in his or her life? What values did the person have with which you would not agree?

89 Help your children set goals for building each of your top values into their lives. Because this is an ongoing process, the goals will be phrased in terms of "Beginning (date), I will ..." Remember that goals must be realistic, measurable, and dated to be effective. Write the goals each child sets on a sheet of paper so you can refer to them over the next several months as the plan takes shape.

Help your children build a more positive self-image in terms of values. Encourage them to share how they see themselves in these areas and how they can improve. Then discuss how these improvements might change their self-image. Help your children paint an exciting and vivid mental picture. Encourage them to ask God's help to become the person in the new picture.

Tell your children stories about how your heroes or your friends came to accept and own specific values. As you read or hear personal stories, take notes that will help you explain your values to your children in terms they can understand.

Create a family values chart. Place values across the top and the names of each family member down the left side. Make copies so you can use one chart each week. As you notice a family member demonstrating a value, put a hash mark in the appropriate square on the chart. Encourage a little friendly competition to see who can get the most hash marks in a week. You also can affirm the person who gets the most hash marks under a particular value or the one who gets hash marks under each of the values. Allow family members to recommend one another for hash marks.

You can teach a couple of different values by challenging your family to a 24-hour fast (dinner to dinner). You will want to do this on a nonschool day, such as Saturday, Sunday, or a holiday. Fasting is a way to exercise self-control and a way to become sensitive to the plight of two-thirds of the world's population who experience genuine hunger every day. You could teach generosity and sacrificial giving by having your children compute the cost of the food the family would normally have consumed that day, then send that amount to an organization that feeds the homeless, cares for starving children, or works to eliminate world hunger. Each time you do this, allow your children to choose which organization will receive the check. This will increase their personal ownership and stake in the exercise.

Teach older children about chastity by asking them to list reasons that young men and women have sexual relationships. Then add to the list any of the following, which they may have not identified:

- to experiment with sex to see what it is like

- to gain self-gratification and personal pleasure

- to feed one's ego by overcoming a partner's objections or winning "the most popular teenager"

- to be accepted by others and not be rejected by one's dating partner

- to express love for another person

- to demonstrate love and commitment

Point out that many of the reasons can be hurtful (such as the first four) and are not good reasons for becoming sexually involved with a dating partner. The last two reasons may be good reasons, but God's plan is that expressing love and commitment through a sexual relationship should be done within a marriage bond.

When watching a television program that indicates a couple is sexually active, living together, or considering sexual relations, ask your teenagers to identify which of the above reasons appear to be the motivation for the involvement. Discuss how the couple might talk through the temptation and arrive at a God-pleasing solution.

Pick bouquets of flowers, add pretty ribbon, and go to a bus or train station. Look for people who appear to be tired, discouraged, or lonely and give them one of the bouquets. This helps children develop sensitivity, kindness, and generosity.

Have your children make a dozen greeting cards that illustrate values such as love, kindness, and courage. Include appropriate Bible verses on the cards. Take these to a retirement center and have the nursing staff direct you to 12 people who have not had visitors or telephone calls in the last year (or month or week). Let your children personally deliver the cards.

Select an agency that works with children and, as a family, sponsor a child. Decide together on things your family will go without—an evening at the movies, lunch twice a week, new clothes, the newest computer game, soft drinks, or desserts several times a month—to save the monthly support amount. Encourage your children to write to the child. When you hear from the child you are sponsoring, make a big deal out of reading and sharing the letter.

98

Make a values chart for each child to review before going to bed. Your children get to check off each value they have demonstrated during the day. Ask your children to think of ways to demonstrate the values the next day. Ask, "How could you show kindness tomorrow?" Pray with each child, asking God to remind him or her to do the things named.

99

Have your children label Tinkertoy building blocks or Lego plastic building blocks with the names of different values. Then each person builds a creative structure. When everyone is done, each person describes what the structure represents. Then ask your children to note which values are connected and see if they can think of ways the values relate to one another. For example, self-control and kindness might be linked. You could say that, when exercising self-control, you often are being kind to others, and when you decide to act in a kind way, you sometimes have to exercise self-control.

100

Using ¼"-thick pieces of Styrofoam plastic foam (cut to size to simulate mortar) and 25 real bricks, build a pretend brick wall outside. Make it at least four rows high. Ask your children to explain the function of real mortar. (Ideas: It holds the wall together, keeps the bricks from rubbing together, and compensates for any uneven surfaces in the bricks.) Next, discuss how values perform the same functions in our relationships with others. (Our values allow us to develop intimacy and bonding. Our values keep us from grating on one another. Our values allow us to accept and understand that no one is perfect.) Ask each child to identify ways that values help make his or her friendships work better.

101 List actions your children will do during a typical week. These may include eating, sleeping, washing dishes, sweeping the floor, doing homework, taking a test, sharing with a friend, going to church, and taking care of a pet. Read from your list and ask your children to identify which (if any) values are being demonstrated by each action.

102 Create a chart that lists people and ways to show respect (or love or kindness) to those people. The list might include: Mom, Dad, Grandmother, Grandfather, friends (by name), teachers, and neighbors. Encourage your children to think of at least five individual, different ways to show respect to each person on the chart.

103 Attend garage sales or flea markets and buy old buttons (not collectibles, just buttons). Give each family member (including yourself) a small cloth bag. Each week choose one value to concentrate on as a family. During the week, each time you notice a family member acting in accordance with that value, give him or her a button to place in his or her cloth bag. Each time you notice someone acting in opposition to the value of the week, remove a button from the bag. Children can give buttons to family members as well. At the end of the week, gather as a family to discuss the many ways you demonstrated the value.

104 Have a Bible verse search. Each child holds a closed Bible. You call out the different verses (from activities 3, 4, 5, 6, 7, 8, 12, and 15 in chapter 1). Your children compete to see who can find the verses first and read them aloud. After each verse, ask your children to say what value is suggested by the verse.

105 Have your children make paper chains from strips of construction paper taped or stapled into circles. On the first link write the name of one of your top-priority values, such as respect. Before adding a link, ask your children to think of what respect leads to, then label the strip for the second link with that attitude, feeling, or action. Continue doing this until you run out of links. Then begin a new chain with a different value. A "respect" chain might have links such as "kindness," "sensitivity," "friendliness," "acceptance," "love," and "relationships." Hang the chains around the family room for a couple of weeks.

106

Ask your children to describe who God is. (Refer to activity 4 in chapter 1 for ideas.) Ask them to describe the persons we will want to become in response to the person God is.

107

Focus on one value each month. At dinner, every family member shares how he or she demonstrated that value that day. This develops a daily habit of demonstrating a value, which after 30 days will be a strong foundation for accepting and owning a particular value. This also gets children in the habit of looking for creative ways to demonstrate values. Affirm each person for his or her positive choices and behaviors.

After several months, revisit values previously emphasized. At breakfast once or twice a week, announce that today you will look for ways to demonstrate a value other than the one your family currently is exploring. This will reinforce for your children the importance of continuing to practice all the values.

108

Encourage your children to show kindness, sensitivity, and friendliness by looking for ways to include other children who are normally left out of activities. To prepare for this activity, ask your children to tell about a time when they were left out and how they felt. Then ask if they have noticed kids who are being excluded from games or activities. (They will probably be able to name several.) Challenge your children to think of ways to include those children and to follow through. Synchronize watches and state that report time will be at 1800 hours (6 P.M.) the following evening. Your heart will be warmed by their stories.

109

Roleplay real-life situations your children may face in school or with their friends. This helps them practice making God-pleasing choices and thinking of the right things to say.

110

Obtain copies from a library of short plays that would be useful in teaching values. Make a copy of the play for each family member. Assign parts and read through the play together—in your best dramatic style. Discuss how the play illustrates your values.

111

After explaining that a parable is a story that makes a heavenly point, read the parable of the Good Samaritan (Luke 10:30–37). Discuss the values illustrated by each character. Then select a different value and have each family member write a short parable illustrating it. Share the parables you have written.

112

Occasionally "bless" your children at breakfast. To bless someone is to predict or ask for God's favor for him or her. Sometimes blessing someone involves "renaming" a person or "reframing" their self-image from inept to competent, from angry to in control, or from negative to positive.

Set the ground rules in advance. If you bless some-one with a specific value for the day, he or she will act on that value for the entire day. So if you say, "Johnny, today I ask God to bless you with an atti-tude of kindness." Johnny reports at dinner how he demonstrated kindness.

113

Give your children a list of your top-priority values. Ask them to name the different ways they have observed you demonstrating those values.

114

Illustrate the meaning of faith and trust for your children. As a family, ask one member to volunteer to be blindfolded and, standing, allow himself or herself to fall into the arms of the family. This calls for faith and trust that the group will catch the indi-vidual and provide support. Take turns (provided you have the necessary people to assure safety) until everyone has been blindfolded. Then share your experiences of how it feels to "step out in faith" and take that fall.

Explain that this activity illustrates faith and trust in God. His Word tells us "faith is being sure of what we hope for and certain of what we do not see" (Hebrews 11:1) and "we live by faith, not by sight" (2 Corinthians 5:7). Use a concordance to look up other passages about faith and trust. Then talk about ways we trust in God in everyday situations. Share experiences where you have trusted God, especially when you had to make values decisions, and how it felt to know His sure hand was on you.

115

Teach your children a simple but straightforward way to share their faith with others. This could be sharing with others that they pray every morning for safety during the day. Or they can invite a friend to attend Sunday school. It might be an explanation for why a specific value is chosen. Children are never too young to point others to Jesus. (See 1 Timothy 4:12.)

116

Sit in a circle. Write sentence starters on individual index cards. Change the value to match your current emphasis. Go around the circle and complete the first sentence, then move on to the second sentence. Continue until each of you has completed all the sentences. Here are some sample sentences using *courage.*

- For me, courage means …
- It takes real courage to …
- The last time I had to act with courage was …
- How I know I need courage in a situation is …
- When I pray for courage, I ask God to …
- A situation this week in which I need courage is …

117

Set up a mock courtroom. One child will be the judge, one child will be the attorney for the defense of a specific value, and another child will be the attorney against that value. The remaining family members (or friends) will be the jury. No witnesses will be called. The attorneys simply will make their best case for (or against) the value. After both attorneys have presented their cases, they may be allowed a rebuttal speech or may debate the case. At a specified time the judge stops the trial and the jury deliberates on which attorney presented the most compelling argument. When they have reached a decision, the jury returns and reads the decision. Then hold a general discussion and critique on how the case for the value could have been made undeniably compelling.

Have your children conduct a survey of your neighborhood or apartment building to determine the top two values held by those surveyed. Have your children list five to eight of your top-priority values and duplicate enough copies to use during the survey process. Your children will ask people to name their top two values. If respondents need prompting, your children can read from the list of values. Compile the results and discuss what the survey revealed about the attitudes of the people in your neighborhood.

Design a wall mural that illustrates your family's values. Work together as a family to paint the mural on an appropriate wall.

Have your children write prayers to God about developing right values in their lives. Encourage them to pray these prayers at least once a day.

121

Show your children a Scripture verse that advocates a specific value. (For example, Ephesians 4:32 for kindness.) Next have them personalize the Scripture verse by rewriting it and including their own names. (For example, "Nate, be kind to others.")

Remind your children often that without the help of the Holy Spirit, we cannot live out any Christian value. Talk about times when you have failed to act according to your values and have asked Jesus to forgive you. Pray as a family, asking God's help in living out the values you discuss.

4 explore the values

"As soon as I'm 16, I'm quitting school," Ernie declared to his mother as he tossed his books on to the kitchen table. "School is just a waste of time!"

Leanne's first thought was to give Ernie a lecture on the benefits of finishing school, but she caught herself. She stopped what she was doing and invited Ernie to tell her more about how he was feeling and what was making him consider school a waste of time. Ernie was only too willing to share his list of grievances with someone who would listen. When he finished, Leanne agreed that he had made some good points. She then asked Ernie to make two lists—one of reasons to finish high school, the other of reasons to quit.

Leanne and Ernie reviewed the list together and discussed each item. Even when Leanne thought some of the reasons were unrealistic, she didn't dispute Ernie's belief in what he had written. However, during the discussion Ernie changed his mind about some of the reasons and altered his list.

Next, Leanne asked Ernie to think of three adults he respected. She asked him to share his list with each of these people and get feedback

*from them within the next few days. She also sug-
gested that Ernie explore the job market for people without high school educations and check his
beliefs with the vocational counselor at school
and with a businessman who was a friend of his
dad's. Ernie agreed to everything.*

*Eventually, Ernie decided for himself that stay-
ing in school was his best alternative. However,
he stayed in school because he chose to, not
because Leanne forced him to.*

VALUES DO NOT develop in a vacuum. They develop through an ongoing process of interaction and exploration and application to real life. The more your children explore values, the more feedback they receive and the more information they have for making wise choices. Discussion and conflict resolution are powerful ways to strengthen one's values.

*To teach his children how to reason things
through, Jack began asking them to come up
with the pros and cons of an issue or decision
they were facing. At age 10, Paul already was
planning to save money for a motorcycle. He
was full of ideas about the good aspects of
motorcycles. When Jack asked Paul to list reasons why buying a motorcycle might be a poor
choice, he was stumped at first. Then, hesitantly,
Paul began to mention rain, no room for passen-
gers, no trunk to carry things in, and danger on
the highways. Instead of arguing with Paul
about whether he could buy a motorcycle, Jack
helped Paul explore both sides of the decision.*

Jack frequently used this technique with his

children. "Tell me four positive things and four negative things about honesty," he would say. And over a period of years he was delighted to see his children learning to think of options, results, and possibilities of making wise choices.

Through the process of considering several options and perhaps even experiencing some of the consequences of the options, children take a particular belief or value and make it their own. Like a classroom teacher, you must prepare interesting lesson plans to help your students explore your values. Use any and every creative teaching method to catch your children's interest in the values you want them to learn. Start with the following suggestions and add your own.

122

Develop a case study, complete with thought-provoking questions at the end. Give a copy to each child. Tell your children that they are a panel of experts that will provide counsel to the characters in the case. Build into the narrative several factors that may influence the behaviors or choices of the characters. As you listen to the discussion, pose additional questions that will encourage your children to consider which values are involved and all the options and consequences.

123

Give your children a roll of light-colored contact paper and permanent markers in several colors. Have them design catchy bumper stickers that illustrate your top-priority values. They can give the bumper stickers to friends or post them in their rooms.

124

Challenge your children to make a values mobile. You will need string, poster board from which to cut out shapes, scissors, felt-tipped pens in various colors, and small dowels for the crossbars.

125

Design and make puppets you can use for teaching about values. You can make the heads from papier-mâché with painted faces and yarn hair. The older your children, the more sophisticated the puppets can be. Younger children may enjoy making animal puppets from socks. Give the puppets names that relate to your top-priority values such as Honest Joe, Loving Linda, Self-Controlled Sally, or Patient Patrick.

Lay the kitchen table on its side so your children can crouch behind it as they perform puppet shows. Give your children a situation and have them act it out for you. Each character must behave in the manner that his or her name suggests. Adding an antagonist, such as Greedy Gus, may provide drama.

126

Work together to develop humorous skits in which people are faced with choices involving values. While the characters may initially make inappropriate choices, they should eventually make the right choice. Take the time to write lines that are truly funny. You may be surprised at the creativity in your family. Design a program that includes two or three of your skits. Practice the skits, then invite friends to watch your family perform. Provide snacks and have a fun evening.

127 Write a sentence about one of your top-priority values and have your children turn it into a rebus. (A rebus is a combination of letters and pictures that conveys a message phonetically.) For example, "Honesty will be my first choice." The rebus might include a picture of a light switch in the "on" position, a bird's nest, a golf tee, a sheet of paper with "Will" written at the top, a bumble bee, the letter *m,* a picture of an eye, a blue ribbon with "First" on it, and a person looking at two desserts. (On-nest-tee will bee m-eye First choice.)

128 Give each child a short list of your top-priority values and a hymn book. Set the kitchen timer for 10 minutes and see who can find the most hymns referring to or reflecting each value listed. When time is up, have your children take turns telling which hymns they found and why they picked each one. Choose two or three of the hymns to sing together.

129 Write a family values song. Older children may make up their own tunes and write the lyrics. Younger children may need to write new lyrics for a familiar tune such as "Happy Birthday." Then assemble a family band and play the song. The band may play a combination of musical instruments or use instruments that anyone can play, such as cellophane on combs or kazoos. Have one family member be the vocalist and sing your new family song. Make a recording of this historic moment.

130 Suggest that your children write poems about your top-priority values. Younger children may select one value and write a short "Roses are red/Violets are blue" poem. Older children may write longer poems that address each value. Use the poems to make greeting cards, plaques, or posters. Print them on your computer using attractive fonts and post them throughout your home.

131 Explain *haiku* poetry to your children. A *haiku* is a poem consisting of three lines and a total of 17 syllables. The first line has five syllables, the second line has seven, and the third line has five. An example would be:

> Honesty for me
> Means being truthful always.
> My word is valued.

Then spend an evening writing *haiku* poems about your values.

132 Design a bar graph for each family member that shows the number of times your top-priority values are acted upon in a typical week. Discuss how long to make each bar on each person's chart. Self-evaluation, as well as group feedback, will be the basis for the decision on the bar lengths. Repeat this exercise at the beginning of each month and note progress as the graphs change.

133

Design and make a stained-glass window for your home that illustrates two or three of your top-priority values. If your children are young, you may choose to make a simulated window using cardboard and colorful cellophane or crayons. A personalized stained-glass window would be an unusual and unique home decoration—one that will provide opportunities for your children to explain to friends the values illustrated by the design.

134

Writing a paraphrase is an excellent learning activity because it forces you to take a thought and put it into your own words. This process also encourages ownership of the idea. Give your children things to paraphrase to help them interact with your top-priority values. Examples include

- Short sentences such as "Honesty is the best policy" or "Courage is acting bravely when afraid";

- Bible verses such as Philippians 4:5 for gentleness, Colossians 3:23–24 for industry, Colossians 3:9 for honesty, or 1 Corinthians 13:1–8 for love;

- fables or stories that teach values; and

- Bible stories.

135

Work together to develop a mission statement or credo for your family that clearly communicates an intention to reflect your values in your words, actions, and decisions. An example might be:

The Johnson family is committed to treating others with courtesy, loving one another, telling the truth, exercising self-discipline, encouraging reasonable risk-taking, and being loyal to one another.

After you have written the mission statement, spell out the ways you will be able to tell if your family is living up to what you have written. Write performance objectives such as "We will be courteous by listening to and not interrupting whoever is talking, by not yelling at one another, by knocking before opening a closed door, and by taking turns."

Post your mission statement and performance objectives where everyone can see and refer to them. When you observe your children meeting one of the performance objectives, affirm them by saying, "You are demonstrating our family mission statement. That's wonderful! I feel excited when I see you doing that!" On the other hand, when you observe your children acting in a way that violates the mission statement, you can call this to their attention and remind them of the appropriate behavior.

Read together the story of Josiah, the boy who became king of Judah when he was eight years old. He reigned for 31 years and was a good king. (See 2 Kings 22:1–23:30.) Ask your children to list all the things Josiah did that made him a good king. Then ask them what characteristics they would consider important for a king to have and why. They should include your values as part of the list. If not, you might suggest these by asking questions such as, "Would courage be important? Why or why not?"

Next, discuss what characteristics you would expect in a president or governor. Finally, discuss how the expectations you have of a king or a president are or are not different from those you have of one another.

137

Simulate a contemporary talk show. Pick a topic for the show that focuses on one of your values such as "people whose best friends lied to them" or "courageous kids." Give your family at least a day's notice of the "show" so everyone can think of personal experiences that fit the topic. You act as the host and family members will be the guests who tell their personal stories. As each person tells a story, ask, "How did you feel when that happened?" and "What were the consequences of that choice?"

138

Challenge your children to design symbols for different values. For example, love might be represented by a heart or a circle (because love is unending). Or honesty might be represented by the word "lie" in a red circle with a red "X" across it. Bake sugar cookies and decorate them with icing using the symbols your children designed.

139

Have your children design a coat of arms for your family that incorporates each of your top-priority values. A coat of arms is often in the shape of a shield that is divided into quadrants. Words and drawings appear in each quadrant. You might encourage your children to draw a ribbon along the outline of the shield and write in the names of the values separated by dots.

If you or one of your children has artistic talent, you might make a black-and-white version of the coat of arms and use it to make stationery for your family.

140 Encourage your children to increase their faith in Jesus by reading to them from the life of Christ as told in the gospels. The miracles of Jesus demonstrate His power, His concern, and His responsiveness to people's needs. The friendships Jesus cultivated reveal His love. And by His life and His words, Jesus points us to God. Jesus modeled self-control as He fasted, courage as He resisted temptation, humility as He prayed, and love when He sacrificed Himself for us.

141 Give each child a personal diary. Explain to your children that each night they are to write how they demonstrated your values by their words, actions, and decisions during the day. Encourage your children to keep the diaries current and honest, and promise them that what they write will remain confidential. You may want to begin a values diary yourself!

142 Buy a blank journal for each family member. Using self-adhesive tabs, divide each journal into sections devoted to one of your top-priority values. Explain to your children that a journal is a place to record

ideas and reflections, important quotations, and observations. Encourage your children to reflect on one of the values in the journal and write their thoughts and ideas at least twice a week.

143

Tape a long sheet of white shelf paper to a wall in the family room. Provide crayons and pencils and tell your children to fill the sheet with graffiti that identifies and illustrates your values. When the sheet is filled, read aloud what was written. Affirm creativity.

144

Read a Bible story that illustrates values. Start with the care of the Good Samaritan (Luke 10:30–37), the courage and kindness of King David's mighty men (2 Samuel 23:13–17), or Daniel's courage (Daniel 6:1–28). Then have each child write a letter as an observer of the incident might have written to a friend. Have your children note the values demonstrated by the different characters. When everyone finishes, read the letters aloud.

145

Select one of your values as the topic for a panel discussion. Give each family member something different to read about that value. You may use poems, song lyrics, quotations, a short section in a book, a magazine article, a newspaper story, Bible verses, or something you have written. Each person has 15 minutes to read what you have given to them and to prepare a short presentation based on the content.

At the end of that time, conduct a panel discussion in which you each take turns making your presentations. Then discuss how all the ideas work together to give a better concept of that value.

146 Assemble a jigsaw puzzle. Spray paint the surface with a light-colored paint such as gray, light blue, or pale green. Next, write the names of all the Christian values you can think of using permanent markers or a small paintbrush and oil paint. Let the paint dry. Break apart the puzzle and save it for a special evening of fun.

147 Tell a continuous story about a brother and sister who demonstrated the values you want to teach your children. First, write several of your top-priority values on small slips of paper and place them in a bowl. One person draws a slip from the bowl and starts making up a story. The person has to include something in the story that illustrates the value written on the slip of paper. After a few minutes, that person stops talking and points to another family member who draws a slip of paper and continues the story. After a few more minutes, the second person stops talking and points to another person to continue the story.

148 Find pictures or sketches that illustrate one of your values. Tape a large sheet of flip chart paper to the wall. Borrow an opaque projector and project the picture or sketch onto the sheet of paper. Your children can copy the picture by tracing the image onto the flip chart paper. After they have completed the picture, take down the paper and allow them to color it with crayons, watercolors, or felt-tip pens. As they color, talk about how the picture communicates the value to each of you.

149

Read *Pilgrim's Progress* by John Bunyan to your children. This is an allegory that your children might enjoy. You will find many of your values illustrated in the book. After you finish a selected portion, stop to discuss the values from that segment.

150

Make a family slide show to illustrate how your family acts on your values. There are a couple of different options for this. First, you might list the different values, then spend an evening looking through slides you already have. Select those that demonstrate your values or that remind you of experiences where your behavior was consistent with your values. Coordinate the selected slides into a complete show with narration and recorded music.

A second option is to keep the camera loaded and take a couple of rolls of slides, one picture at a time. When you catch a family member acting on your values, snap a picture. When you have enough slides, arrange them into a slide show with narration and music.

A third option is to agree on how each value could be demonstrated by actions, then pose for the slides.

The slides could then be coordinated into a slide show.

A fourth option is to go to a busy place, such as a mall, and actively look for people doing things that illustrate your values.

151 Make a family values video. Spend an entire evening (or more than one, if necessary) planning the script. You can include many of the projects suggested by the activities in this book—posters, poems, presentations, skits, songs, and banners. The video could be a series of skits, one long original play, a combination of presentations by family members, or a little of each. Once you are satisfied with the script, gather the props and costumes and begin filming. Have fun!

152 Assign a specific value to each child as a research project. Your children may use any number of options for gathering information to make the final presentation on the project. For example, they might conduct a survey, design a quiz, note references from the library, draw pictures, include photographs, or interview friends. Give a realistic deadline and plan an appropriate incentive for completing the projects—a family outing to a favorite theme park, a party for friends, a vacation day with your children doing all their favorite things.

153

Write a choral reading about one of your values, then have the family read it aloud in unison. This could be a personal prayer for help in developing the value, similar to David's prayer in Psalm 19:13–14.

154

Use the Scripture verses from activities 4, 5, 6, 7, 8, 12, 15 in chapter 1 to develop a mix-and-match quiz for your children. List the Scripture references down the left side of a sheet of paper and the different values from those verses in a second column. Have the children look up and read the verses, then draw lines from the reference to the appropriate values in the other column.

155

Work together to develop a "life map" for a Bible character. Each event in the story is added to the map, which you design to look like a road map. Indicate where the character may have taken a detour, gone the wrong way, or slowed down because of wrong decisions. Show how God brought the individual back on track, making progress toward becoming a more mature man or woman of God.

156

Watch and record a television program for later viewing with your children, or watch a prerecorded movie, and write questions for your children to answer after viewing it together. Select an appropriate time when you can watch the program without interruption. Give different questions to each child with instructions to read the questions before the program begins and to be prepared to answer the questions after it ends. The questions should lead children to look for behaviors that demonstrate values and the results of making either good or bad decisions about those values. Ask, "How did Susie show that she was loyal?" "How did Peter demonstrate courage?" "What did Amy learn about the consequences of lying?"

157

After Sunday school, ask your children to tell you the Bible story (younger children) or main points of the lesson (older children). Encourage them to tell as much as they can remember, including all the details. Whenever possible, point out the specific values being taught by the story or how the lesson topic relates to values. Listening to a lesson is one part of the learning process. Retelling it is another way to increase learning and understanding.

158

Ask your children to tell you what they enjoy about going to church. If there are things you can do to enhance their enjoyment, be sure to do them. If attending church is a positive experience for your children, they will be more likely to continue actively participating in the church community.

Things that might make church attendance positive include encouraging children to invite friends, helping children participate in the worship service by sharing a hymnal or pointing out key points of the service, stopping for a donut and a glass of milk on the way to church, or having a second Sunday school in the afternoon so your children can teach you what they have learned.

159 List the Ten Commandments (Exodus 20). Post these close to the television. Each time you watch television together and see one of the commandments kept or broken, challenge your children to identify which one it is. This exercise not only teaches children the commandments, it helps them develop the voice of conscience to remind them they should keep God's commandments.

160 Have your children contrast and compare the values of two characters in a story in terms of values, decision making, and life consequences. Some of the pairs in Scripture you might use include the two sons in Matthew 21:28–32; the younger and elder brothers in the story of the prodigal son (Luke 15:11–32), Mary and Martha (Luke 10:38–42), and the rich man and Lazarus (Luke 16:19–31). Look through your children's favorite storybooks for other character pairs to compare and contrast.

161 Plan opportunities for your children to practice your values. For example, when you bake cookies (or any other dessert), make an extra batch for your children to take to a friend to encourage sharing. Rather than merely contributing to the food pantry at church, make up entire food baskets and deliver them as a family to teach charity. Celebrate May Day by having your children make paper baskets, fill them with flowers, and hang them on the neighbors' doorknobs to teach kindness. Keep a couple of snow shovels in the garage (if you live where there is snow!) and after a big snowfall, take the kids and shovel the neighbors' walkways. (If you live in a sunny climate, you can keep brooms and sweep walkways after a heavy wind.) Keep an eye out for older individuals you can help in this way.

After any of these experiences, share how you feel when you do the right thing. Ask your children to express how they feel about themselves and what they did. This links good feelings to making God-pleasing choices and acting on values.

162

Spend time during dinner telling your children about your experiences with God, particularly those stories that demonstrate His provision, protection, and guidance. Your faith and stories from your experiences can be powerful stimuli for your children's faith development.

163

Have your children write television commercials for two or three of your top-priority values. Then have them perform the commercial with you as the audience.

164

Someone once said, "Children are fragile, handle with prayer." You can never pray too much for your children. Spend time each day praying for each family member, asking God to help them accept and own your values. When you pray at mealtimes, include a short request about values. Say, "Help each of us to look for, and take advantage of, opportunities to be kind." Encourage your children to begin praying at an early age, asking God to help them become loving, kind, courageous, etc. When you pray with your children at bedtime, include your request that God will help your children develop a sensitivity to values that please Him and that He would help them make choices that please Him. So your prayers don't become routine, focus on different values on different days and change the wording of your requests.

165

Have your children write a lesson plan to teach a specific value. Teachers have long known that they learn the most when they are preparing to teach a lesson.

166

Follow David's example in Psalm 119:11 and establish a memorization schedule for the family. Identify specific Bible verses you want your children to "hide in their hearts" to keep them from sin. Set a goal to have your children memorize at least 100 verses before they are 10 years old. (That's only two verses a month from age 6 to 10.) Whatever is memorized during those years tends to become a lifelong memory. Some people find that they can recall verses they memorized as a child better than those they memorized later in life. Do whatever it takes to encourage your children to memorize Scripture. The benefits of having your children know the Scriptures are without price. Consider offering a special reward, not only when verses are first memorized but also if the verse can be repeated at a later time when the reference is given.

167

When you read a local newspaper story about a person who demonstrates one of your values in a significant way, have one child contact the person and ask for a personal interview. Work together to develop questions that will help bring out the value behind the behavior or decision. Take your child to the interview location and sit through the interview too. Afterward your child can report to the rest of the family. An older child could write a short magazine article about the story and submit it to an appropriate editor for consideration.

168

Give each child a small notebook and a pen. Tell them they are detectives who must find clues to other people's values. Take them to the mall and set a rendezvous time to pick them up. They are to wander through the mall, making notes of any clues they see to the values held by shoppers. For example, a demanding customer arguing with a store clerk might indicate a lack of self-control, selfishness, or even dishonesty ("I never wore this blouse. I insist on returning it!"). Someone pushing a person in a wheelchair might reflect kindness.

169

Work with your children individually to develop a training plan that will help them learn some of your values. This would be particularly effective with values such as self-control, courage, thrift, and perseverance, though it can work for any value. Examples of what to include in the training plan include gathering information about the value from a variety of sources, identifying behaviors that demonstrate the value, acting in accordance with the value, feedback, and evaluation. Once the plan is developed to your mutual satisfaction, implement it.

170

Buy a toy medical kit and label it "Dr. Value Fixer." Explain to your children that whenever you see one of them behaving inconsistently with your values, you will take the stethoscope from the bag, place it around the appropriate neck, and hand that child the bag. You will say, "Doctor, your honesty (or any other) value is broken. How can you fix it?" This will be a signal for the child to take a quiet time-out to consider how to make appropriate value-related behavior changes. When your child has an acceptable plan, he or she shares it with you, ends the time-out, and puts the medical kit away.

171

While your children are babies, begin collecting stories of their experiences. They will love to hear these stories as they grow older. You can use these stories to reinforce values by telling and retelling those which demonstrate one of your values. The best way to keep track of these stories is to write them down no later than the end of the day on which they occur. Despite good intentions, many parents don't make time to do this. A second option is to keep copies of letters you write to friends or family in which you tell stories about your children. A third alternative would be to tape record the account as quickly as possible. If you don't keep track, you will find that you forget many of the touching moments and cute conversations.

Plan a values treasure hunt. Select a value as the focus of the hunt. Write clues to hide in the house, yard, or neighborhood. Each clue has two parts—a clue to find the next clue and a one- or two-word clue to the selected value. Give copies of the first clue to all participants. (You may need to stagger start times by several minutes so participants follow the clues, not one another.) Participants try to guess the value from the second part of each clue. The "treasure" should be hidden in your home so the hunt ends up back at the starting place. The "treasure" is a slip of paper with "Congratulations! You found me. I am (the value)." You also might include treats for everyone who finds the treasure.

Have your children design and draw a cartoon strip that illustrates a specific value. Select and name the main character of the strip. Make the strip a monthly project, focusing on a different value each month.

174

Send your children to the library with instructions to find as many resources as they can about one of your values. (Hint: You can use these resources in your role as teaching parent.)

175

Have your children do an Internet search on values in general or a specific value you want to teach. Print appropriate articles and add them to your family values scrapbook.

176

Select a specific value and identify a related behavior you can practice for a week. Sometimes the behavior might be the same for all family members; at other times it will be different. For example, you might focus on developing courage and not letting fear control your behavior. Younger children might agree to practice going to bed without a night-light. Teenagers who are terrified of rejection might choose to practice asking different people for a date. You may decide to practice confronting people about issues of concern in your relationships. Each day, share how the practice sessions went and how you feel about developing courage.

177

Buy a supply of play money to use when teaching your children about self-control and patience. On payday, give each child the same amount of play money as your net paycheck. Then every time you pay a bill, tell your children which bill and how much it was. Each child returns that amount of play money to you. When you go to the grocery store, show your children the receipt and collect that amount of money. Whatever you spend is matched by the play money returned from each child.

When a child wants a new toy or wants to purchase a special item of clothing, evaluate your budget. Tell your child you will put aside a certain amount of money each payday to save for the purchase. Be sure to do so. Give your child an envelope labeled with the name of the desired item. He or she can put the same amount of play money into the envelope as you save from your paycheck. This way, your child can see the savings grow until there is enough to pay for the item. When the item is purchased, your child returns the play money. If there is money left over at the end of the month, discuss what happens to the "extra" money.

178 Help your children develop financial responsibility, self-control, patience, and good decision-making skills by giving them an allowance to cover specific expenditures. Younger children may get to buy their own snacks. Older children may be responsible for managing a clothing allotment. You can ask them to pay for their own entertainment activities from the allowance.

It is important that rules be applied consistently. Parents who rescue children by giving them extra money when they run out of allowance are not only failing to teach good values, but they also are teaching their children that irresponsibility gets rewarded and consequences can be avoided.

Ask your children to share a problem they have with another person. Then work together to develop a resolution that is consistent with your values. Think of ways to deal with issues honestly, demonstrate loyalty, act courageously, and do it all with kindness. Evaluate the pros and cons of each idea. Let your children decide which approach they will take and when. Invite your children to report back to the family on the results. If the results were less than satisfactory, encourage them to try another approach.

Encourage your children to develop good decision-making skills. One way is to let them make some of the decisions when grocery shopping. You can set the parameters of the decisions: "Which of these three desserts shall we buy?" "Which of these green vegetables shall we buy?" "What fruit do we want?" Making decisions that have mealtime consequences is good practice for children. This helps them understand that decisions always have consequences.

Older children can learn to make thrifty decisions by using coupons, comparing price per ounce, and checking the price differences between cuts and kinds of meats.

Do a "force field analysis" exercise. The theory behind this approach to problem solving is that the status quo has equal forces pushing for and resisting change. One way to move the status quo in a desired direction is to increase the reasons and rewards for positive change. This works well for short periods, but soon the energy to support the extra effort will diminish and the status quo will slip back to where it was. Another method to move toward desired change is to remove some of the obstacles and reasons to resist the change.

Write the name of one of your values at the top of a sheet of paper. Then draw a line horizontally across the middle of the paper. Label the line "Where we are right now." Brainstorm a list of reasons or forces that push your family to become *more like* the value. Draw arrows from the bottom of the page up to the line and label these arrows with the different reasons you listed.

Next, brainstorm a list of the reasons or obstacles that keep your family from moving toward the value. Draw arrows from the top of the page down to the line, and label these arrows with the items you listed.

Discuss any other reasons or incentives you can add to push the status quo line upward. Then discuss ways to eliminate some of the obstacles or negate some of the forces that hold you down. When you do this, the pressures become unequal and the status quo changes more easily.

182

Have your children describe how they would act or be known if they were truly the most (name the value) person in the world. Ask, "What would you do or how would you be known if you were the most honest person in the world?" Children might respond in a variety of ways.

- I'd never tell a lie.

- Everyone would know they could trust me.

- I'd keep my promises.

When they have exhausted their ideas, ask, "How could you be like that now?"

183

Encourage your children to take Jesus' advice about going a second mile and doing more than is requested (Matthew 5:41). Help them see that being extra nice to others can make a big difference in relationships. Discuss recent situations when your children were kind or responded positively to a request. Ask what might have been an appropriate "second mile" in those situations. The more examples they can come up with, the more likely your children will be to recognize future opportunities to be extra kind.

184

Have a family filibuster night. The object is to respond to your questions in as many different ways as possible in 45 seconds. Use a stopwatch as a timer. Point to one child and ask, "What does it mean to be (name the value)?" The responder must talk for the full time and must stop when time is up. Select a different value each time you point to someone and pose the question.

185

Think of several situations when your children might be called on to make difficult decisions about values. Pose the situation and ask, "Which of your friends would help you make the right decision?" and "Which of your friends might push you to make the wrong decision?" Sample situations include being offered a copy of the questions on a history test, being pressured to accept or use drugs, not wanting to leave a fun party to make it home by curfew, or being tempted to lie about who hit the baseball that broke a neighbor's window.

186

Help children to learn to follow their conscience when faced with temptation. When they share with you about an incident where they have faced temptation, ask, "What is/was a God-pleasing way to act in this situation?" Share James 1:5–6 with them to assure them that if they ask God for wisdom, that the Holy Spirit will give them guidance.

187

Some people divide values into two groups: those you are and those you give to others by your behaviors. Select one child and one of the giving values (kindness, love, loyalty, dependability, friendliness, unselfishness, sensitivity, respect, justice, or mercy). Instruct all family members to demonstrate that value toward the identified child for the entire day. At the end of the day, the recipient evaluates the efforts and explains how each person demonstrated the value.

188 Teach your children to choose God-pleasing behaviors without receiving external affirmation or praise. (See Matthew 6:2–4.) Induct them into a "secret service" organization. The goal is to do kind things for others without letting anyone know who did it. The immediate reward is the positive self-image one develops. As your children practice this, they will become more skilled at recognizing their internal reward system. They will be more likely to act in ways that help them maintain positive self-esteem.

189 In the book *In His Steps* by Charles Sheldon (Pyramid Books, 1960), the lives of the people were changed when they began to ask themselves "What would Jesus do?" and began to behave in the same way. Make small cards with that question on them. Laminate a copy for each family member to carry in pockets or purses. If older children are afraid they will be ridiculed by friends for carrying the card, then put only the initials of each word on the card— "WWJD?"

Share stories of how that question helped you make the God-pleasing choice and behave consistently with your values.

190 Have your children write and present stylized scenes from a favorite story that emphasizes one or more of your values. Use costumes and take pictures or make a video of the tableau.

191

Take every opportunity to affirm God at work in your children's lives. For example, when they tell you the truth regardless of the consequences, say, "Wow! I can see God is helping you become an honest person. I love it!"

5 model the values

"Don't forget to let your children know that you love them. Don't just tell them, show them love by your actions." Vicky told a friend.

VICKY WAS RIGHT. Every day she deliberately demonstrated her love to her children. As she stacked freshly laundered clothes on her daughter's bed, Vicky placed notes saying, "I did your laundry because I love you and want you to have clean clothes." She frequently included notes, funny cartoons, and little cards in her children's lunches. She prefaced her "Good morning" to her children with "I love you."

When we tell our children about values, we are competing with everyone else's messages, and sometimes our children are not even listening. When we model our values, we hope and pray that our children are watching. Some are; others are not. Some children grow into adulthood with contradictory values and inconsistent beliefs and behaviors. Children may easily be enticed into points of view and actions contrary to our desires. Parents could despair of teaching values at all. But we must never stop teaching with our words and our actions.

It's important that parents communicate their values to children through role modeling. If your actions are consistent with your words, the message is reinforced. However, when there is a discrepancy between what is said and what is modeled, the message is usually ignored.

Therefore, you need to model the values you want to teach your children. In fact, look for creative ways to demonstrate your values and, when necessary, call attention to what you are doing so your children won't miss it.

Think of yourself as a visual teaching aid. Be aware that children do watch to see how you handle life, problems, people, and challenges. Keeping this thought uppermost in your mind, you will have an incentive to live consistent with your values. In the process, these values become even more integrated into your life.

Here are some suggestions for modeling your values.

Demonstrate generosity, stewardship, and commitment to the Lord with regular gifts and offerings. The Old Testament standard of a tithe of 10 percent is a good guideline. On payday, announce, "Another paycheck! The first thing I'm going to do is write a check to the church. I always pay God before I pay anyone else."

Contribute to a mission project each month, even if it is a small amount. Talk about the project with your children. Say, "I want to do my part to help bring the Gospel to people who have never heard about God. That's why I send my offering each month."

If you receive extra money (an overtime paycheck, an inheritance, or someone repays a loan you made), consider giving an extra gift to your mission project. Tell your children, "I'm so excited that we got this extra money. Now I can send more to our mission!"

Set aside a few hours each month to be a volunteer. Make this time inviolate. Don't let any other demands keep you from your commitment to give this time to others. There are opportunities in every community. Hospitals, retirement centers, nursing homes, literacy programs, prisons, charitable organizations, and your own church all can use volunteers. It is often more helpful to select just one, learn the routine, determine where you fit in, and become a dependable worker. If possible, involve your children in volunteer work at the same place and time as you serve. Tell your children how good it feels to know you can show kindness to people by volunteering.

A short-term mission trip is an excellent way to teach older children about being grateful for all they have, how to be kind and helpful to others, and how to be a willing and industrious worker. As your children see you getting up early and working hard all day without getting paid, they will note your commitment to many of the values you are trying to teach. And as they work alongside you, they can participate in the excitement of the project. At night say, "I am so tired, I could sleep standing up. But I feel so good because we are able to show love and kindness by helping these people."

Find organizations in your city that serve meals to the homeless and use volunteer help. Take the entire family to help serve a meal. On the way to and from the meal, talk about what it would be like if you lost your home and all your possessions. Ask what would be frightening or uncomfortable. Talk about the challenges of being homeless. On the way home, discuss the experience and how your children feel about being kind and helpful. Doing this several times can help your children observe your sensitivity to others and encourage them to become more sensitive themselves.

If you and your children go grocery shopping and notice someone with a sign that says "homeless and hungry," take this opportunity to model sensitivity, kindness, and generosity. In addition to the groceries you need, buy a loaf of bread, a small package of lunch meat, an apple, and a can of juice. Ask the clerk to bag these items separately. Give the bag to one of your children and say, "Did you notice the person with the sign that said 'homeless and hungry'? What would it be like to be homeless and hungry? Let's show a little generosity. Give this bag of groceries to the person."

Bring your annual performance appraisal home from work and share it with your children. Discuss how the good ratings please you because you give your best on the job. Point out ratings or comments that are consistent with the values you teach your children. Supervisors often use words such as dependable, punctual, reliable, conscientious, meets deadlines, and accurate. These and similar words are easily tied to values.

Also acknowledge those ratings that are lower than standard or comments about areas in which you need to improve. Say, "I have to work to improve in these areas." Then share specific things you will do.

When you are reading a book or newspaper and one of your children wants to talk with you, put aside what you are reading. Say, "I don't want anything to distract me while we talk because I love and respect you. I wouldn't want to be discourteous or rude to you."

Keep a list of your top-priority values where you can refer to it easily. Every day find ways to demonstrate each of those values, and make sure your children notice. For example, when you prepare your income tax returns, be honest. Only claim legitimate deductions. Share that with your children. Say, "Sometimes I feel tempted to include deductions that I know are not legitimate. But that wouldn't be honest, so I don't do that." Or if you are going to ask your boss for a raise and feel nervous about it, say, "I am anxious about talking with my boss. What if my request for a raise gets turned down? What if my boss becomes angry with me? You know, my stomach is a little upset just thinking about what might happen. I'll have to ask God to help me do this anyway. I'll have to be courageous."

When you fail to live up to your values you can use the experience as a teaching tool by acknowledging that you need to work on the value violated. For example, when you lose your temper with or around your children, say, "I just lost control didn't I? I'm sorry. I will work on improving my self-control."

202 During family devotions, confess to God those shortcomings you need to work on. Ask for God's help in becoming more like Christ, especially in the areas of your values. You also can demonstrate love, kindness, gentleness, and forgiveness in your prayers for others and for each child. If you don't pray aloud with your children, you are missing a terrific opportunity to model your values.

203 Be quick to apologize to or in front of your children. Practice different ways to say you are sorry and to ask for forgiveness. Be sincerely contrite and be sure your tone of voice communicates this. Closing your eyes and praying aloud, "God, I was wrong. I am sorry. Please forgive me." is an additional reinforcement. This also shows your children that behavior toward others has an impact on our relationship with God.

204 Show forgiveness by your actions. Don't hold grudges. Don't assume that because someone hurt or disappointed you, there is malicious intent toward you. Give the benefit of the doubt. Be the first person to initiate reconciliation with others after an argument. When someone apologizes, offer forgiveness and risk trusting that person again. Will you get burned sometimes? Yes. It's that kind of world. People let one another down. And we all need to be forgiven frequently.

Let your children know that, sometimes, it isn't easy for you to forgive. You might say, "That was some argument I had with my friend George. We both said things we probably didn't mean. And he truly hurt my feelings with what he said about me. Part of me doesn't care if I ever speak to him again. But that's not the part of me I want to listen to. I am going to go over to George's house right now and tell him I care about our friendship. I'll ask him to forgive me and I'll forgive him. That's the right thing to do."

Demonstrate honesty by telling the truth yourself. Don't lie to make someone feel good. Don't lie to get yourself out of commitments. Don't lie about being sick when you don't want to go to work. Don't exaggerate when telling stories. Just tell the truth.

Model ways to act lovingly toward others. Include the children in planning ways for you to show love. At breakfast ask, "How could I show my friend Sarah that I care about her?" Then do some of the things your children suggest and report what happened.

Let your children see you act in a self-reliant manner. Make home repairs. Take care of your needs rather than asking someone else to bring you a glass of iced tea. Tackle challenges with a "can do" attitude rather than complain or look for someone to rescue you. If you want to know how to do something or to learn a new skill, do the necessary research, take lessons, and do what it takes to learn.

208 Obey the laws. This means no speeding or illegal U-turns and no paint cans in the regular trash. It means participating in mandatory recycling programs and keeping your dog on a leash. Parents who routinely disregard the law will have a hard time convincing their children not to use drugs because it is against the law. (Of course, that isn't the most important reason not to use drugs, but parents generally mention the law when speaking about drug use.)

209 Model submission, responsibility, and obedience by following the rules. There are rules at work, in church, in most organizations, and even in games. When you don't exempt yourself from rules, you reinforce for your children the importance of their obedience to the rules. When you discuss the rules for your family, point out that you not only make rules (for the family) but also have to follow rules made by other people. Explain that you don't like all the rules you must obey (or make), but that you choose to be obedient.

210 Make it a habit to look for kind deeds to do. Help a neighbor. Assist a friend with a project. Do thoughtful things for your children. Work on a community project. Run errands for an older person who no longer drives. Cook a meal and take it to the pastor's family. Look for the good in others and in situations rather than focusing on the negatives. Be ready with a kind word for people. Kind words lighten the mood. They cheer, encourage, and affirm.

211

Monitor your leisure reading so your children don't see you reading inappropriate magazines or books. Not only is this right for you, but it witnesses to your children how to guard one's mind from sinful input.

212

Demonstrate honesty by giving back the extra money if the checkout clerk gives you too much change. Turn in a lost wallet to the police. Tell your children what you did unless they were with you. If they are with you at the time, be sure they hear you say, "You gave me too much change. I want to be honest. I only gave you a ten dollar bill not a twenty."

213

Watch your language. Don't use sexist language. Don't make racial slurs. Don't use curse words. Don't tell inappropriate jokes, and don't laugh at one told by someone else. Don't use God's name as an epithet. If you slip up, quickly apologize and say, "I don't want to be the kind of person who talks like that. I will work harder at speaking appropriately."

214 Set priorities. Life is full of conflicting demands. There is always more work than you can accomplish. You may find that you are frequently out of money, energy, or time. You can be a good model for your children by setting priorities and focusing on the top priorities in each area of your life. Involve your children in the priority-setting process. List all demands or chores you are facing and decide which can be eliminated and which can be done less frequently. Get organized. Use good time management.

215 Show your children what your priorities are by how you spend your time. Look back over the last week. How much time did you spend doing things with your children or with your spouse? How much time did you spend in prayer or reading the Bible? How much time did you spend watching television? Consider how you might restructure your time to reflect your priorities. Compute how much discretionary time you have each day. For example, if you deduct the number of hours you sleep (8); you work (9); you commute (1.5); you prepare, eat, and clean up after meals (2)—then you have 3.5 hours left each day. Decide how to make that time count with your family.

216 Demonstrate financial responsibility. Would you feel comfortable with asking your best friend or your children to read your checkbook and see how you spend your income? Your children can tell what is important to you by how you spend your money. Do you pay a monthly fee to a health club but never use it? Do you rush out to buy the latest model car, television, or stereo when the one you have is still in good condition? Do you spend a lot of money eating out? Do you have more clothes in your closet than you need?

217 Model the kinds of relationships you want your children to develop. Show them that friendship requires attention, patience, and work! If you are married, treat your spouse the way you would want your children to treat their spouses. Be the friend you want your children to become. Demonstrate loyalty, honesty, love, sensitivity, justice, mercy, and all the values that you tell your children are important to you.

218 Develop credibility with your children and the other people in your life. If you state a fact, be sure it is true. If you are not sure, preface your comment with that information. If you don't know something, admit it rather than bluff. When your children rightly call you on being unfair, acknowledge that fact and do what is necessary to be fair. You don't have to always be right to be credible, you just have to be willing to acknowledge when you are wrong.

219 Tell your children about your personal heroes. Say what you admire about them, how they inspire you, and how you try to emulate them. Point out the values those heroes demonstrate in their lives. Whom you admire says a lot about who you are and what you value.

220

Demonstrate integrity. Your children need to see that you are the same in any situation and with anyone. In other words, don't behave one way at church and another way at home. Don't talk one way with non-Christian friends and another way with Christians. If you tell your children to always do their best in school, then you must always do your best at work and at home. When your walk matches your talk, you have integrated your values into your life. You have integrity.

221

When you need guidance from the Lord for a particular decision, or wisdom for resolving a problem, or divine intervention in something over which you have no control, share this with your children. Pray together. Ask your children to pray for you in this situation.

When you make the decision, resolve the problem, or see that God has intervened, share this with your children and give the praise to God for answering your prayers. In this way you can show your children that you believe in prayer and that God does respond to your requests.

222

Attend Sunday school and church with your children. Parents who just drop off their children or send them to church with neighbors are sending a message that church isn't important or relevant for adults.

223 Be a generous tipper. After a nice meal in a restaurant, say, "I am going to give our waitress a generous tip today. I appreciated all her hard work in serving us and making sure our drinks were refilled." In this way you model generosity and gratitude.

224 Actively look for things your children are doing right. Affirm those behaviors. This lets children know that you notice when they behave according to your values. It also gives them ideas about behaviors you consider to be good and important. And it encourages children to do more of the right things. It is more effective to catch children being good and affirm them than to see them doing wrong and criticize them.

When affirming behaviors, state the behavior, affirm the child, praise the behavior, and tell how you feel when you see that kind of behavior. Say, "You shared your favorite toy with your friend. I'm proud of you. Sharing is a very nice thing to do. When I see you share, I feel happy."

225 Share with your children Scripture verses and thoughts from your personal devotions. Tell them why that thought or verse seemed particularly meaningful to you. Let them hear how you apply scriptural truths to your everyday life and relationships. When you can share how a verse in your morning devotions addressed the exact situation you faced that day at work, you show your children that the Word of God is applicable to today and that God guides you through His Word.

226 Do a family Bible study. You can purchase study materials from your local Christian bookstore or develop your own lesson plans. You might do a topical study with older children to see what God says about chastity, sexual intimacy outside of marriage, and marriage. Studying the Bible together shows your children that you value the Word of God and find it interesting and relevant. This encourages them to read the Scriptures on their own.

227 Tell your children about your spiritual journey. Be open about your personal relationship with God. Share some of your struggles and how God is strengthening you spiritually. Demonstrate your faith by not giving in to the temptation to worry about things you cannot control. Explain how your faith has been tested and how that same faith got you through some tough times. Tell about your spiritual "mountain top" experiences. Acknowledge any doubts God has helped you overcome.

228 Be polite and courteous toward your family members. If you are going to the kitchen for a glass of milk, ask if anyone else wants something. Open doors for your children if you see that their hands are full. Before you change the channel on the television, ask if anyone minds if you do so. When your children are on the telephone in the kitchen or family room, remind everyone else to keep the noise level down.

229

Let your children see you go to the Bible to find answers for problems or challenges in your life. (You may do this even when you already know what the Scriptures say.) For example, if your children are aware that you and one of your friends or neighbors has had a disagreement, you might announce, "This situation is not good. I'm going to read what the Bible says about situations like this." Then turn to Matthew 5:23–24 and read it aloud. Then say, "I guess I will go talk with my friend and resolve this problem."

230

If you are watching television or a movie that takes an immoral or amoral approach to one of your values, either change the channel or turn off the television. Explain to your children that you do not approve of the message the program or movie was giving.

231

Be consistent in your application of house rules and consequences. Don't have an absolute rule that bedtime is 8 P.M. and make an exception because you are having friends over and you don't want to go through the usual bedtime arguments. Or, if you do not allow eating in the living room, don't ignore the rule when you are too tired to go to the dining room table. Although exceptions can be made occasionally, the rules need to be clear and consistent so your children know exactly where the boundaries are.

232

Keep your word even when you don't want to do so. Children need to know that you mean what you say. Your word should be the same as a promise. If you make a commitment, follow through. If you agree to do something, do it. If you tell the children you will take them bowling on Saturday, take them bowling.

233

Take walks together. Walking is both an excellent exercise and a good opportunity to talk. Don't take along the cellular telephone so you won't be bothered by calls. You will be able to focus on your children and what you are seeing. A walk in the woods lets you experience the beauty of God's creation and to comment about how much you appreciate that beauty. Take time to pray during your walk, thanking God for making such a wonderful world.

234

Demonstrate respect for your children. Knock before opening a closed door. Say "please," "thank you," and "excuse me." Listen attentively. Avoid teasing, mocking, or belittling your children. Ask for input and feedback. Act on their suggestions when appropriate. Include your children in planning family vacations or major expenditures.

235

Ask your children to be private detectives assigned to watch you for a one-week period. They are to make notes on your behaviors. They will write down the behaviors that demonstrate the values you teach and the behaviors that seem to be in opposition to those values. At the end of the week, your detectives will submit their reports. Accept the feedback gratefully. Thank your children for helping you become aware of the ways you demonstrate your values and the ways you send conflicting messages.

Whenever possible *ask* your children to do what you want them to, don't *order* them. Say, "I want you to take out the trash. Would you do that for me in the next 15 minutes?" Some children may respond by saying "no" or "I don't want to" or "I'll take it outside before I go to bed." You could exercise your parental power and order them to take out the trash immediately. A better alternative is to consider negotiating. As long as the trash gets taken outside sometime during the evening, your goal has been achieved. If you receive a "no" or an "I don't want to," explore the reasons. Ask, "Are you saying you don't want to take out the trash right now, or in the next 15 minutes? Would there be a better time later this evening?" If that doesn't work, say, "As long as you take the trash out before supper (watching television or bedtime), it will be okay. But the trash must go out tonight."

It may take practice to make it a habit to ask rather than order—and still get your children to do what you want. Keep working at it because it will make a positive difference in your relationship with your children. A "thanks for taking care of that" will go a long way toward building mutual respect.

237

Show respect by encouraging your children to make choices. When it is time to make a decision, give them a choice of two alternatives that are acceptable to you. This gives practice in making choices and makes children feel they have control over some things. For example, say, "It's 7:30 and bedtime is eight o'clock. Do you want to play for another 15 minutes, then take your bath? Or do you want to take your bath, then play until bedtime?" Or say, "Here are two dresses that are appropriate for church this morning. Which do you want to wear?" Or say, "Thanks for helping me with the dishes. Do you want to wash or dry?"

You can eliminate some of the power struggle arguments by using this technique. This approach allows children to choose from acceptable alternatives, which makes them feel included. It also gives young children lots of practice in making decisions—something most adults learned in later adolescence or young adulthood.

238

Be sensitive to your children's feelings. Don't talk about their problems to your friends in front of your children. There may be a good reason to seek advice from a friend, but do it privately and ask your friend to keep the information confidential. If your children feel that you are telling everybody about their problems, they may feel betrayed and less inclined to share future problems with you.

239

Keep confidences. Don't tell secrets that people have confided in you. Your children need to know that you are a safe person to share issues they are not willing to share with others. If the secret is one that should be shared with the police or the parents of the other children involved, you will need to talk through this with your children. If you feel you must share the information, explain why you feel so strongly. Explain that you would want to know if your own child were involved in a similar situation. Try to persuade your children to accept, or at least understand, why you must share. However, such situations are probably rare. You are generally safe if you keep to yourself what your children tell you in confidence.

Respect your children's personal privacy. Don't read diaries or journals without permission. Don't listen in on telephone conversations. When you are making rules about your privacy, remind your children that you respect their privacy and tell them how you do that.

Obey the rules you set for your children at home. If children aren't allowed to eat in the living room, then don't eat there yourself. If children are not allowed to snack before dinner, then don't come home and have a snack. If you make a rule that your older children must let you know where they are going and when they will return, then reciprocate. When you go out, say where you are going and when you expect to return. If you require children to telephone if they are going to be late, then you should do the same. When parents follow the same rules they expect their children to obey, children see how important the rules are. You become a good role model.

242

Demonstrate attitudes toward money that are consistent with your values. Some people have poor attitudes about money. These include the following:

- I use money to get even with others.
- I consider tithing unnecessary because I don't live under the law.
- I use money to reward myself with expensive gifts.
- It's my money. I earn it. I have a right to spend it any way I want. If I need more, I borrow.
- My spending habits are no one's business but my own.

Instead, remember that God gives us money to take care of our families, to support His work, to help others, and to prepare for future emergencies and retirement. With this in mind, put God first, avoid borrowing whenever possible, make payments on time, prepare for the future, buy only what you need, wait for sales, and spend your money to the glory of God.

243

Always actively study or learn a new skill. This is one way to model the importance you place on learning. You may study a foreign language that will help you in your neighborhood or work, a new skill for doing things around the house, a sport that requires skill, a musical instrument, or learn more about computers and the Internet.

244 Evaluate your debts. Make a commitment to get out of debt as soon as possible, with the probable exception of your mortgage. Charge accounts can be paid off if you attack the numbers systematically. Make a chart. List your creditors and the current balance at the top of a sheet of paper. Write the months down the left side. For each month, indicate the minimum monthly payment required for each creditor. After creditors, include monthly expenditures such as rent, food, gas, utilities, church donations, and any other usual expenditures. Attack the smallest bill first. When it's paid off, use the amount of money you paid on that bill to increase the amount you pay on the next smallest bill. Keep following this principle until all your bills are paid off. You will find that your bills will become more manageable in a fairly reasonable amount of time, as long as you don't add new debt.

Share the chart with your children, express your excitement at getting out of debt, and work toward an "everything paid in 30 days in cash" mentality. Make a commitment not to jump back into debt.

245 Demonstrate delayed gratification, patience, and responsibility by refusing to be an impulse buyer. Go shopping with lists (grocery, clothing, shoes, books, etc.) and don't buy things that are not on the list or that are not essential to everyday cooking, your wardrobe, or library. If you see something you truly want, either substitute it for something you were planning to buy or add it to a "later" list.

246 Use a 30-day list. When you or your children want to purchase something, add it to this list. Nothing is purchased immediately. What happens during the 30-day waiting period often is interesting. Some children become more convinced that this is exactly what they want, and the item stays at the top of their list. Others find something they want more and put that at the top of the list. Some find that they are no longer interested in the original item and want it removed from the list. The same things may happen to items you put on the 30-day list. This is a good way to demonstrate patience, responsibility, decision making, and delayed gratification.

247 Teach your children how to shop by comparing quality, price per unit, warranty, nutritional value, shelf-life dating, and comparing the cost of prepared food versus food you prepare yourself. When the car needs an oil change, have one of your teenagers call around to find the best price. This teaches that prices differ greatly in the real world. It lets your children see just how much can be saved by taking the time to make a few telephone calls.

248 Take time to compliment people on things they do. This may be the secretary who brought you the cup of coffee, the typist of the error-free report, the busy waiter at lunch who served your lunch quickly, the man who let you merge into the lane you needed to use to exit the interstate, your child who brought you a glass of water, or any number of people whom you might notice but do not normally take the time to affirm. Stop. Take the time. It's important. Your kids are watching.

249 Write appreciation notes. Be known as the card person. Find inexpensive cards that you can purchase in bulk. (I found new, very nice cards for 25 cents each at a General Nutrition Center. I bought 75!) Keep a supply of different kinds of cards on hand to send to friends at appropriate times. You can find some lovely cards that have no message so you can write a personal thought. When you hear that someone is having a bad day, send a card of encouragement. When you hear that someone did well, send a congratulatory card. When you just want to reach out in love, send a card.

If you can't find affordable cards, then use postcards, make your own greeting cards, or write letters or short notes of appreciation and support.

When appropriate, involve your children in selecting the cards and writing the messages. They also can help deliver the cards in person.

250 Write letters of appreciation at every opportunity. These can go to your doctor, nurse, waitress, salesclerk, a friend, your children, your spouse, one of your children's teachers, or the plumber who did such a good job of clearing out the sewer lines at your house. The list is endless. If you develop a thankful heart, you easily could say "thank you" 50 times a day. You may want to design a small card that says "Thanks for extraordinary service. I want you to know that I noticed and appreciated what you did. Keep up the good work." Give your children a few of these cards and encourage them to recognize people who show they have values consistent with your family's.

251

When an older relative or friend begins telling stories about you from your childhood, you may feel embarrassed. Rather than remaining embarrassed, listen to the story, relate it to a value you want to teach your children. Explain how you did or did not act in accordance with that value. Tell how you felt when you acted as you did. Say how you would handle a similar situation today—especially what you would do differently.

6 teach values with bible stories

"When I first started teaching my children about values, I mostly lectured to them," Chad admits. "It seemed to me that I had to look a long time to find examples from real life to illustrate those values. Then a curious thing happened. I began to notice more and more examples. I mean, it was as if I developed a values awareness. Everywhere I went, I saw people demonstrating their values. Try it, it works! Then I found I was reading the Bible with an eye for stories that taught values, and I discovered there were a lot I could use."

YOU WILL WANT to use Scripture as the basis for teaching your values. This ensures that your children understand that your values are distinctively Christian. Teaching from the Bible gives a spiritual dimension to the values you are emphasizing. You can emphasize that when children develop values drawn from Scripture, they will be pleasing to God and conforming to the image of Jesus Christ. A child's faith, like ours, is strengthened through hearing and reading the Word of God (Romans 10:17). Linking values to Bible stories makes them more than entertainment for children.

As you use Bible stories to teach and reinforce values, the Holy Spirit will be at work. He will strengthen your children's relationship with the Lord. Your children will learn to live out their faith through practicing Christian values.

In addition to applying values from Bible stories to everyday experiences, remember to be a model for valuing the Word of God. Let your children see you having personal devotions. Instead of having only your children memorize verses, you memorize along with them. Talk openly about the Bible, your personal experiences with God, the sermon from Sunday morning, and how your faith influences your decisions. Initiate discussions that will stimulate your children to understand and accept spiritual values.

Examples of values that you can teach from Bible stories are included in this chapter. Following each Bible story is a suggestion for using other activities in this book in conjunction with that story. Feel free to exercise your own creativity and mix and match other activities.

Remember a very important point: You are teaching values when you use these Bible stories—not the way of salvation. The characters (except Jesus!) all had their faults and sins. It was God who remained faithful to them, and they had faith in God. The desire to uphold values is the desire to please God and respond to Him because He is faithful. In everything He does—from sending Jesus to be our Savior to providing our daily food—God shows His faithfulness. Our faith in God and in our Savior Jesus Christ, brought and strengthened by the Holy Spirit, is what brings our salvation—it is God's work, not our efforts to earn it.

252 Teach obedience and forgiveness with the story of Adam and Eve in the Garden of Eden (Genesis 2:15–17; 3:1–24). This story clearly illustrates the importance God places on obedience to His commandments *and* His all-encompassing love that, even when Adam and Eve disobey, provides a plan for their redemption. (See Genesis 3:15, which refers to the coming work of Jesus as Savior.)

This story provides experience with the Law and its consequences and helps to explain the sinful nature that we inherited from our first parents, Adam and Eve. Law always needs to be countered with the Gospel that "God so loved the world that He gave His one and only Son, that whoever believes in Him shall not perish but have eternal life" (John 3:16). Emphasize that Jesus paid for the consequences of our sinfulness and that the Holy Spirit is at work through God's Word to help us overcome our sinful nature.

Also point out that God expects people today to keep His commandments (John 15:10). Reinforce this truth and show that God also wants people to obey governmental laws and the rules set by parents as you read Romans 13:1–3 and Ephesians 6:1–3.

Someone will likely ask, "If God forgives, why is it so important for us to be obedient?" One part of the answer is that we want to be obedient because God loves us so much and we want to please Him (John 14:15). You also might study Romans 6:1–14, which addresses this subject. We are able to work at being obedient, not because we fear the Law but because we have been united with Christ.

As an activity, have your children draw pictures of Adam and Eve being forced from the garden. This will help them visualize the price of being disobedient. Then have them draw a picture of people celebrating because Jesus, through His suffering, death, and resurrection, brought eternal life—an entry into a new Garden of Eden that is heaven.

253

Teach respect for others and self-control with the story of Cain and Abel (Genesis 4:1–15). You also can use this story to illustrate the consequences of disobedience (nonacceptance), jealousy, anger, and murder. Read Jesus' comments about hating someone in Matthew 5:21–22 and Paul's comments about forgiveness and love in Colossians 3:13–14.

Have your children rewrite the story of Cain and Abel in a couple of different ways. In the first rewrite, Cain will bring an acceptable sacrifice to God. In the second rewrite, Cain still brings an unacceptable sacrifice, but he repents instead of being angry when God does not accept it. This helps children see the other choices Cain could have made.

254

Teach obedience, faith, courage, patience, and gratitude with the story of Noah (Genesis 6:11–9:17). Noah was obedient even when God gave him an incredible task. There had never been a flood such as the one God said was coming. Noah exercised his faith in God by gathering the animals and moving his family into the ark seven days before any rain began to fall. It took courage to move into the ark without ever testing it to be sure it would float. Noah and his family had to exercise patience while waiting for the rain to end and the earth to dry out enough so they could leave the ark. Noah and his family showed God their gratitude by offering a sacrifice when they left the ark. Read Genesis 9:11–16 so your children can see that God is faithful. He gave us rainbows to remind us of His promise never again to destroy the entire earth with a flood.

Using a cardboard box as a base, build an ark with a removable top. Cut out shapes for the different animals and birds. Place them in the ark. Draw and cut out figures to represent Noah's family. Make a large rainbow for the wall. Encourage your children to use the ark and rainbow to share the story with friends.

255 Teach peaceability with the story of Abraham and Lot (Genesis 13:1–9). Show that the fighting between the shepherds who worked for Abraham and Lot caused so much trouble that the family decided to separate. Show how generous Abraham was to let Lot have first choice of where to live. Point out that Abraham and Lot could have joined in the quarrel, but they found another way to settle the problem—a way that resulted in peace.

Have one child write a page from Abraham's journal for the day he and Lot separated. Have another write a page from Lot's journal. Read and compare what they write. Read the New Testament admonitions for us to be peacemakers in Matthew 5:9; 1 Thessalonians 5:13; and Hebrews 12:14. Discuss the implication of "blessed," "loved," and "be holy."

256 Teach perseverance with the story of Abraham the intercessor (Genesis 18:20–19:29). Abraham interceded with God for the people of Sodom until God promised not to destroy the city if there were as few as 10 righteous people living there. Because there were not 10 righteous people, God destroyed the city, but He remembered Abraham and sent Lot, his wife, and his daughters out of the city. (But Lot's wife looked back and became a pillar of salt.)

Read Philippians 4:6 for a New Testament instruction to make our requests known to God through prayer. Have your children share experiences when they prayed to God several times with a specific request and He answered by granting their request. An example might be to help them study well and remember the information they needed for a test on which they later received a high grade. Think of experiences you can share to illustrate perseverance.

257

Teach faith, faithfulness, obedience, and courage with the story of Abraham and Isaac (Genesis 22:1–19). Abraham was told to offer as a sacrifice to God his son, Isaac, the one through whom God had promised to make a great nation. Abraham had such faith in God that he proceeded to obey. What courage it took to consider offering his beloved son whose birth was a miracle from God! When Isaac asked where the sacrifice was, Abraham replied that God would provide. And God did stop Abraham from killing Isaac, providing a ram for the sacrifice. Because of Abraham's faith, God promised to bless him.

Compare this story to the sacrifice of Jesus on the cross. Jesus was God's beloved Son, yet God did not spare Him from dying for us (John 3:16; Romans 8:32). Look for hymns that illustrate the values in this story and sing them together. Examples include "Trust and Obey," "Where He Leads Me," and "I Will Follow Jesus."

258

Teach goodness, friendliness, helpfulness, hospitality, and kindness with the story of Isaac and Rebekah (Genesis 24:1–67). When Abraham's servant asked Rebekah for a drink of water, she freely gave him one, then offered water for the camels. She even suggested that he and the camels come to her house for lodging. Verses to couple with this story include Galatians 5:22–23 and 1 Peter 4:8–9. Have your children invite a few friends over and show them full hospitality.

259

Teach honesty and unselfishness with the story of Jacob, Esau, and the birthright (Genesis 27:1–40). Point out how unscrupulous, selfish, and dishonest Jacob was in what he did. Have your children identify the consequences Jacob suffered because of his actions.

This would be a fun story for your children to dramatize. Let them write the script and find props and costumes. You become the audience for the performance. Then read what Paul says about unselfishness in Philippians 2:3–4. What is the motivation (Philippians 2:5–11)?

260

Teach love and perseverance with the story of Jacob and Rachel (Genesis 29:1–28). Show how Jacob demonstrated his love by his actions and was willing to be patient for seven years to marry Rachel. When her father tricked him by giving him Leah as a bride, Jacob promised to work another seven years if he could marry Rachel. Have your children draw a cartoon strip illustrating this story.

Read what Hebrews 6:9–12 says is the reward of patience. Discuss ways your children can practice perseverance and patience. Remind them that their faith and patience work hand in hand.

261 Teach unselfishness, kindness, honesty, courage, faith, industry, dependability, chastity, and forgiveness with the story of Joseph (Genesis 37:1–36; 39:1–47:11). Describe how Joseph's brothers were jealous of him and how they plotted to get rid of him. Point out the consequences of their cruelty and dishonesty. Use the points of the story to show how Joseph had courage to build a life in a strange country, kept his faith in God, worked hard, was dependable and trustworthy, as well as able to resist sexual temptation.

Help your children understand how hard it must have been for Joseph to forgive his brothers for all that had happened to him. Talk about the source of Joseph's strength. Was it something that only came from within himself or did he have help? Tear out pages about Joseph from a Bible story coloring book and make copies to color. As your children color, discuss Ephesians 4:29–32; 6:10–18.

262 Teach courage, dependability, and kindness with the story of Moses in the bullrushes (Exodus 1:1–2:10). Moses' mother was courageous, his sister was dependable, and Pharaoh's daughter was kind. When Miriam took the responsibility for watching Moses, and getting her mother to nurse the baby, she was helping her mother with a problem. Compare this with Galatians 6:2. Have your children write a letter that Pharaoh's daughter might have written to a cousin about finding Moses and deciding to keep him.

263 Teach courage and faith with the story of the spies sent into Canaan (Numbers 13:1–14:38). Ten of the spies convinced the Israelites not to enter the land God had promised to give them. Because of their lack of courage and faith, these spies and the Israelite adults never got to Canaan. From that generation, only Joshua and Caleb (the spies who gave the good report) were allowed to enter Canaan.

What does Romans 8:31–32 say to us when we feel as if we are standing alone in the right and everyone else is against us? "If God is for us, who can be against us?" Too bad the Israelites didn't believe that. Have your children make a collage representing situations they might face today that would require courage and faith.

264 Teach gratitude and obedience with the story of the serpent of brass (Numbers 21:4–9). Point out how ungrateful the Israelites were after all God's miracles. Also read John 3:14–16 and discuss how Jesus linked that event with His own death on the cross.

Have your children make fiery red serpents from clay and use yellow clay to make a "brass" serpent. Using a small stick, hang the "brass" serpent on a pole. Talk about your project. Was it the brass serpent that actually healed the people? What do we learn about God's love for us?

265

Teach resisting temptation and obedience to God's leading with the story of Balaam (Numbers 22:1–24:25). Balaam did not appear to be tempted by the wealth Balak offered him to curse Israel, but Balaam wanted to please Balak and was tempted to disobey God. God got Balaam's attention by speaking through his donkey! In the end Balaam spoke a blessing on Israel because he decided to be obedient, not because it was what he wanted to do.

Ask your children to write a modern parable in which God speaks to a child through an animal. Ask them to identify ways that God has spoken to people through the ages and how the Holy Spirit speaks to us through the Word today. (See Hebrews 1:1–2.) In the past God sent angels; made personal appearances (for example, Genesis 17:1–22); spoke in dreams; communicated through priests, judges, prophets; spoke from heaven; and talked through the Bible, through Jesus, and through the prompting of the Holy Spirit in our hearts.

266 Teach the values of the Ten Commandments with the story of the giving of those commandments (Exodus 20:1–17; Deuteronomy 9:7–10:5). Show how important these values were to God, so important that God wrote them on stone tablets with His own hand. Then read Matthew 22:35–40 where Jesus says that loving God and loving one's neighbor as one's self is the essence of all the commandments. Ask the following question for each commandment: "How does this commandment relate to loving God or others?"

267 Teach courage, leadership, and obedience with the story of Joshua and the Israelites entering Canaan (Joshua 1:1–5:12). God's message to Joshua was to be strong and courageous (1:6). Because Joshua obeyed God, Israel finally made it to the Promised Land. Compare God's exhortation to Joshua with Paul's instruction to Timothy in 2 Timothy 2:1–7. Both were to be strong in the Lord and a leader or teacher of others. Their strength came from the Word of God. Ask your children to write a prayer of thanksgiving the Israelites might have prayed when they finally arrived in the land of Canaan.

268 Teach respect for the power of God with the story of the conquest of Jericho (Joshua 6:1–27). God caused the walls of Jericho to fall so the Israelites could enter the city. Compare the response of the people of Jericho to the response of the disciples to the demonstrated power of Jesus in calming the waves. They were terrified. They said, "Who is this?

Even the wind and the waves obey Him!" (Mark 4:41).

Have your children write a newspaper story that might have run in the *Israelite Free Press* or *The Fisherman's Times* about these two incidents.

269

Teach justice with the story of Achan (Joshua 7:1–26). Achan tried to hide the wrong he had done, but because of his disobedience the entire nation suffered. God knew what Achan had done, and He directed Joshua to find and punish Achan for disobeying God's instructions not to take anything from Jericho. Read Numbers 32:23, which says, "Be sure that your sin will find you out." Discuss what happens when we try to hide what we have done wrong.

Share a story from a television show or a personal experience in which someone did something wrong and got into more trouble trying to hide it than if they had admitted it. A lie is a good example: Usually if you start with one lie, you end up telling more to cover up the first.

270

Teach courage and faith in God with the story of Gideon (Judges 6:11–7:25). Gideon started with 32,000 men to fight Midian. But God told him that was too many. When Gideon told those who were afraid to go home, 22,000 men left. That could have weakened Gideon's courage. But God said that 10,000 was still too many men. Another 7,000 were eliminated from the army. With only 300 men and some trumpets and lamps inside pitchers, Gideon exercised his faith in God by waging a nontraditional battle. God gave the victory to Gideon.

Young children love to roleplay the choosing of Gideon's army. Older children might do a television news broadcast, interviewing a soldier from Midian and one of Gideon's soldiers. God does great things with small beginnings. Remember the multiplying of the loaves and fishes? Paul learned that God's power is made strong in our weakness (2 Corinthians 12:9).

271

Teach obedience and self-control with the story of Samson (Judges 13:2–16:31). Samson was a physically strong man, but in other areas of his life he did not demonstrate strength. He did not always exercise self-control. For example, he became involved with a woman who betrayed him to the Philistines.

Self-control is one of the fruit of the Spirit listed in Galatians 5:22–23. And Christians are urged not to become romantically yoked with those who do not share our faith (2 Corinthians 6:14). Invite your children to make a coat of arms that illustrates self-control.

272

Teach loyalty, dependability, industry, generosity, and kindness with the story of Ruth (The Book of Ruth). Ruth's loyalty to Naomi is legendary, quoted by Christians and non-Christians alike. Boaz' generosity and kindness to Ruth was unusual. He told his workers purposefully to leave handfuls of barley and wheat for Ruth. Ruth was industrious in obtaining food for herself and Naomi, a dependable daughter-in-law. What does 1 Thessalonians 4:11–12 say to us about being industrious? Ask your children to think of catchy slogans that communicate one of the values from this story and use them to make bumper stickers.

273

Teach courage with the story of David and Goliath (1 Samuel 17:1–58). David could not believe that the Israelite soldiers tolerated Goliath's mockery. He faced the giant with only a slingshot and five smooth stones. With God's help, David killed the giant and became a national hero.

Have your children make slingshots from *Y*-shaped sticks and large rubber bands. Let them target practice with a large bull's-eye in the backyard. Caution them to use these toys only in a safe manner and never to hurt an animal or person or to break an object.

Read 1 Corinthians 16:13–14, which encourages us to demonstrate the courage and strength David had from God. What does it mean to "do everything in love"?

274

Teach love, loyalty, and friendship with the story of David and Jonathan (1 Samuel 18:1–20:42). Jonathan went out of his way to protect his friend, even when King Saul, his father, wanted to kill David. Jonathan even risked the king's anger and punishment because he loved David and was loyal to him. Compare this story with Jesus' love for His friends in John 15:12–17. Then read John 13:34–35 to see Jesus' command that we love one another, the mark of a Christian. Have your children make a poster about friendship.

275

Teach about respect and forgiveness with the story of one of the times David spared King Saul's life (1 Samuel 19:1–25). Even though Saul had repeatedly tried to kill him, David chose to respect the king and not to kill him when he had the opportunity. Instead of acting in anger and revenge toward the person who was trying to kill him, David tried to show the king he was in no personal danger. When Saul realized that David had spared him, he repented of his anger and blessed David.

Proverbs 15:1 says that a soft answer turns away anger, but a harsh word stirs it up. Have your children list ways to give "soft" answers to defuse the anger of others.

276

Teach generosity, unselfishness, hospitality, and goodness with the story of the widow of Zarephath (1 Kings 17:1–24). Although the widow only had a little bit of food, she was willing to share it with the prophet Elijah. Compare this with the description of the early church in Acts 2:42–47. Plan three generous acts you can do as a family and do them within a week.

277

Teach humility and obedience with the story of the healing of Naaman (2 Kings 5:1–19). Naaman didn't want to do what Elisha told him to do to be healed. He felt it was beneath him to bathe in the muddy Jordan. But Naaman's servants urged him to be obedient. As a result of his obedience, Naaman was healed.

Have your children write a poem that Naaman might have written to remind himself not to let pride keep him from doing what God asks. Read what Paul wrote about submitting to one another in Ephesians 5:21–6:9.

278

Teach courage and loyalty with the story of Esther (The Book of Esther). It took great courage for Esther to go to see the king without being summoned. She could have lost her life. But her loyalty to her people, the Jews, gave her courage to do what needed to be done. Because of this one young woman, a plot to kill all the Jews in the country was averted.

Have your children write a page from Esther's diary for the night before she visits the king. Tell them to express her personal fears in what they write and her conviction that she was doing the right thing. Read and memorize 1 Corinthians 15:58, which tells us to be steadfast and always abounding in the work of the Lord.

279

Teach courage, self-control, and resistance to temptation with the story of Daniel (The Book of

Daniel). From the very beginning, Daniel is courageous. He stands up for what is right. Even when threatened with death in a lions' den, Daniel stayed with his convictions and prayed to God three times a day.

When we are tempted, God will provide a way of escape (1 Corinthians 10:13). Have your children make a chart of temptations they face on a regular basis. In the first column, write the temptation. In the second column, list the possible escape routes God provides.

280

Teach obedience, self-control, and mercy with the story of Jonah (The Book of Jonah). Point out the consequences of Jonah's initial disobedience, then his anger when God spared the city of Nineveh. Show how God gave Jonah a lesson about mercy in the last chapter.

Jesus said, "Blessed are the merciful: for they shall obtain mercy" (Matthew 5:7 KJV). Have your children discuss mercy in terms of forgiving behavior. Agree to exercise mercy all week and report back on what happened and on other people's responses.

281

Teach humility with the story of John baptizing Jesus (Matthew 3:1–17; Mark 1:1–11). John felt he was not worthy of the honor of baptizing Jesus. John demonstrated his humility, but Jesus insisted, showing His own humility. Ask your children to write a definition of humility. Then check a dictionary to see how close they came. Ask them to list behaviors that would demonstrate humility.

282 Teach courage of conviction with the story of the temptation of Jesus (Matthew 4:1–11). Ask your children to describe, in their own words, what Satan tried to get Jesus to do. Have them look through several newspapers for stories of people who gave in to temptation. If possible, also look for stories about people who demonstrated courage of conviction and did not give in to temptation.

283 Teach preparedness with Jesus' story of the two houses built on different foundations (Matthew 7:24–29). Give your children Lego plastic building blocks and have them build a small house. Use the white brick pieces to form a foundation. Discuss how values form the foundation for withstanding problems in life. Ask, "How does God strengthen our faith foundation?"

284 Teach faith, trust, and courage with the story of Jesus stilling the storm (Matthew 8:23–27). Then read John 14:1 where Jesus told the disciples to believe in Him. Talk about the fears each family member has. Make a colorful felt banner about the values in this story.

285 Teach sensitivity to the Holy Spirit and openness to God's Word with the parable of the sower (Matthew 13:1–23, 36–43). Encourage your children to study the principles found in Scripture and the values you are teaching them from the Bible so they can be "good growing soil" for truth.

Prepare several different planting containers. One can be empty to simulate the wayside. One can be shallow and have more pebbles than soil. One can be planted with grass seed. And one can have lots of good potting soil. Scatter chive seeds in the empty container and plant chive seeds in the other containers. Place the containers outside. See if you can get the same results as the sower in the story. (The birds may not find the first container and the grass may not choke out the chives, but your children should be able to get a good idea of the story from the experiment.)

286
Teach faith in God's power with the story of Jesus feeding the five thousand (Matthew 14:15–21). As you discuss the power of Jesus to multiply the food, also point out His care and concern for the basic needs (hunger) of the people. Jesus was moved by compassion for the people. To help develop their sensitivity, discuss with your children the problems of hunger in the world. Volunteer as a family to serve food at a shelter that provides meals for the homeless.

287
Teach love and loyalty with Jesus' story of the lost sheep (Matthew 18:11–14). Take your children to a petting zoo. Let them pet the sheep and lambs. While they are doing this, say, "Jesus told a story about a sheep like this one." Tell the story of the lost sheep. This will help them better visualize the story. Emphasize how the shepherd cared about each sheep. Also emphasize how Jesus is our Good

Shepherd because He came to find and save us lost sheep. Have your children think of ways to show love or loyalty to their friends during the next week.

288 Teach mercy and forgiveness with Jesus' story of the forgiven debtor who refused to forgive others (Matthew 18:21–35). Talk about grievances family members may have against one another, things they may not have forgiven. Agree to practice forgiveness within the family, beginning with some of these issues.

Demonstrate how small problems are more easily forgiven one at a time than if they are allowed to accumulate. Give each child a wooden match. Ask them to break it. This will be easy. Then tightly bind 50 matches with a rubber band. Ask your children to take turns trying to break the bundle.

289 Teach generosity and unselfishness with the story of the rich young ruler (Matthew 19:16–26). Point out how some people let greed or selfishness keep them from making wise choices. Take your children to an orphanage so they can donate some of their clothing or toys. (To make this a truly generous and unselfish act, the clothes should be ones they can still wear and toys they still like and use.) Affirm them for their generosity and unselfishness.

290 Teach humility and unselfishness with the story of the mother of James and John (Matthew 20:20–28).

Jesus used this occasion to emphasize that humility is the most honorable choice. Work together to develop a motto about humility and unselfishness and have your the children draw a rebus to illustrate it.

291 Teach goodness, kindness, and sensitivity with the words Jesus will say on Judgment Day (Matthew 25:31–46). Help your children understand that when we help others, we really help Jesus. Talk about times during the past week when you have observed family members showing kindness. Make a food basket for a needy family and deliver it together or ask your pastor to deliver it.

292 Teach about faith, humility, and loyalty with the story of Jesus healing the centurion's servant (Luke 7:1–10). Emphasize the loyalty of the centurion's Jewish friends who did as the centurion asked and pleaded with Jesus to help the sick man. Show the humility and faith of the centurion. Note that Jesus was "amazed" by such faith. Pray together, asking God to strengthen an "amazing" faith in you and your children.

293 Teach preparedness with Jesus' story of the building of the tower (Luke 14:28–30). Use the story to discuss how important it is to plan to make wise choices in tough situations. This might include planning how to refuse to take drugs or planning ways to respond to a repeated offense, such as a sister who "borrows" clothes without permission. Being pre-pared helps one make the right decision rather than acting on impulse.

Have your children draw a design for a small tower built with bricks. Then give them insufficient sugar cubes (or blocks) to complete the tower. Next have them determine how many more cubes are needed to make the tower match the design. Give them exactly that number of cubes. If they can complete the tower, they planned well. If they still don't have enough cubes, or if they have too many, they didn't plan well.

When Jesus told this story, He was explaining that following Him involves thought and planning. We will encounter times when it won't be easy to be dis-ciples of Jesus. We will experience troubles. But with Jesus as the foundation, the "building" of our Christian life will remain strong.

294

Teach gratitude with the story of Jesus healing the 10 lepers (Luke 17:11–19). Explain that not every-one remembers to thank God for His blessings or to thank other people for the kind deeds they do. In this story only one of the lepers who were healed returned to thank Jesus. Challenge your children to follow the example of this one grateful person. Have your children make thank-you cards and write notes of appreciation to relatives, teachers, and friends for things they have done or for demonstrating Christian values.

295

Teach perseverance and repentance with the story of Zacchaeus (Luke 19:1–10). When Zacchaeus couldn't see Jesus because he was too short, he ran and climbed a tree. That's determination! And when Jesus went to his house and talked with him, Zacchaeus repented of his past and demonstrated this repentance by giving half of his wealth to the poor and promising to return four times the amount he had cheated from people. Explain that in repentance, Jesus helps us "turn our hearts around," turning away from the sinful action and asking His help in standing firm against temptation.

Give your children a series of situations and have them tell you which demonstrate repentance and which do not. Examples might include

- A friend uses your bicycle without permission. He apologizes then takes it again the next day.

- A friend teases you about your freckles. When you say you don't like being teased, the friend apologizes and never teases you again.

296

Teach justice and obedience of the law with the story of the question about taxes posed to Jesus (Luke 20:19–26). Talk about the kinds of laws you and your children must obey every day. For the next week, point out instances when you obey the law. Examples might include crossing the street with the "walk" sign, obeying the speed limit, recycling trash, or keeping the dog on its leash. Pray for government leaders who will make just laws and look to God for guidance.

297

Teach generosity with the story of the widow's mite (Luke 21:1–4). Discuss the difference between giving a small amount of what one has and giving sacrificially. Talk about the ways your family gives both from abundance and sacrificially. Agree to give sacrificially to a worthwhile cause. This might involve giving up desserts, sodas, snacks, or movies for a month and sending the amount not spent on these things to an organization working to eliminate world hunger.

298

Teach love, goodness, generosity, kindness, and respect with the story of Mary washing Jesus' feet (John 12:1–8). Point out that even though Mary's deed was generous and good, the disciples grumbled that she should have spent her time and money helping the poor. Jesus explained that Mary was using the perfume to prepare His body for burial. Talk about the reality that others may grumble or tease us when we are kind, but Jesus reads our hearts and thanks us for sharing His love with others.

Surprise a neighbor by doing something nice and totally unexpected, such as mowing the lawn, shoveling the snow, or raking the leaves. Talk about how good it feels to do something for someone else.

299

Teach courage through the power of God with the story of Peter (John 18:15–27; Acts 2:1–41). Compare and contrast the Peter who was afraid and denied knowing Jesus with the Peter who boldly stood and proclaimed the Gospel to thousands. Ask, "What made the difference?" If they don't know, read Acts 1:8 where Jesus promised that the Holy Spirit would give the disciples power. Emphasize, too, that Jesus forgave Peter for his denial and that Jesus will forgive and help us when we fail to live out our witness for Him.

Have your children make creative name tags (or nameplates for their doors) that illustrate areas of their lives in which they feel the Holy Spirit helps them share God's love in powerful ways.

300

Teach generosity, sensitivity, gentleness, and compassion with the story of Peter and John healing the lame man (Acts 3:1–11). Point out that the man wanted money, which Peter and John could not give because they didn't have any. What they did give the man was so much better. They healed the man through the power of the Holy Spirit. When we think of giving to church, a mission, or the needy, we usually think of giving money. But children don't usually have much money to give. This story is one way to help children see that there are other ways of giving. They can give what they have: time, energy, talents, empathy, and love.

If your children are older, plan a family servant event and work to build, clean up, or restore buildings or play areas. If your children are younger, help them take balloons to nursing home residents who rarely have visitors.

301

Teach about honesty with the story of Ananias and Sapphira (Acts 5:1–11). Talk about the consequences of lying. Point out that Ananias and Sapphira lied when they kept some of the money for themselves, not just to people but to the Holy Spirit. Help your children design a poster with the words of Psalm 19:14. Pray together, asking God to keep your words and actions honest.

302

Teach forgiveness with the story of Stephen (Acts 6:1–7:60). Stephen's last words, "Lord, do not hold this sin against them" (Acts 7:60), sound very much like Jesus' words from the cross, "Father, forgive them, for they do not know what they are doing" (Luke 23:32). Stephen learned forgiveness from Jesus' example and was able to forgive even as he was being stoned to death.

Have your children write a report to the leaders of the Jewish community about this incident from the viewpoint of Saul, who witnessed the stoning and watched the coats for those who threw the stones.

303

Teach faith, repentance, and courage from the story of the conversion of Saul (Acts 9:1–29). Contrast Saul's proclamation of the Gospel with the description of his behavior in Acts 8:1–3. Discuss how genuine repentance includes turning away from wrong behaviors and adopting right behaviors with God's help.

Have your children do a character analysis of Saul before conversion and Saul/Paul after conversion.

Research the meanings of the names "Saul" and "Paul." See how they apply to the before-and-after person. Emphasize the perfect life Jesus lived in our place and His sacrifice on the cross to pay for the times when we fail to live out our faith.

304

Teach acceptance, inclusiveness, respect, and goodness with the story of Peter's dream (Acts 10:1–48). Explain that until this time the Gentiles were not being evangelized, only the Jews. Jewish law and tradition held that Jews did not interact with Gentiles. Yet God sent Peter to share the Gospel with Cornelius—a Gentile—and his family. The response was tremendous. This family believed the Good News that Jesus gave His life for them and were filled with the Holy Spirit. Now people all over the world can hear Jesus' saving Gospel proclaimed.

Talk about how, throughout history, some groups of people have been prejudiced against other groups and, in some cases, have done them great harm. Consider African slaves, the Holocaust, the cheating of Native Americans, and the racism that still exists in our country today. If your children are old enough, rent a video that portrays an incident in which prejudice is demonstrated. Discuss questions such as: How did one group mistreat the other? What effect did this have on the mistreated people? What effect did this have on those doing the mistreating? How would you describe the attitudes of both groups? Ask God to help you share His love with all people.

305

Teach self-control, dependability, and justice with the story of the Philippian jailer (Acts 16:16–34). The prisoners could have escaped, but that would have been against the law. Paul and Silas urged everyone to abide by the law, even though the gates were wide open. The jailer, not used to such dependability, was ready to kill himself before his superiors found out about the escape. But Paul stopped the jailer's suicide and explained that all the prisoners were still present. Then Paul shared the Gospel, and the man and his family became believers.

Give your children small notebooks in which to record instances when they feel they are demonstrating self-control or dependability. Remind them that such times often can provide opportunities to share the Good News of Jesus.

306

Teach courage of conviction despite tremendous opposition with the story of Paul at Ephesus (Acts 19:11–20:2). Paul's preaching that man-made gods are not gods at all threatened the lucrative income of the Ephesian magicians and image-makers. Discuss the pressure Paul and the disciples must have felt and the fear they may have felt when the whole city became angry with them. Point out how God protected Paul and the other Christians through the calming words of the city official.

Tell a story from your own experience when you shared your faith, even though you were uncomfortable about doing so. Pray together that God will always keep you bold in standing up for Him.

307

Teach preparedness, honesty, goodness, and faith with the description of the armor of God (Ephesians 6:10–18). It is believed that Paul wrote to the Ephesians while in prison. Paul may have looked out his door and noticed a Roman soldier in his armor as God directed him to record this illustration. When God outfits us with the righteousness of His Son, we are ready to boldly live out our faith by doing kind deeds and by being helpful, sensitive, merciful, forgiving, and friendly. Let your children make the different pieces of armor from construction paper or aluminum foil and cardboard.

308

Teach about love and sacrificial generosity with the story of the Philippian Christians' gift to Paul (Philippians 4:10–19). This church was the only one who supported Paul in his time of need. They didn't have extra to give, but somehow they managed to send enough to help Paul. Plan a project so your family can help support a missionary or a needy child.

309

Teach about repentance, forgiveness, and intercession for a friend with the story of Onesimus (The Book of Philemon). Onesimus had robbed his master, Philemon, and run away. However, Onesimus met Paul, heard and believed the Gospel, and repented of his sin. He was ready to return to Philemon. Paul wrote a letter of intercession for Onesimus, asking Philemon to forgive and accept Onesimus as a fellow Christian. Remind your children that it is the forgiveness Jesus won for us that turns us into "useful" people in God's kingdom.

310

Teach faith and courage with the stories of the family of faith (Hebrews 11:1–39). Review each story and discuss how God strengthened the faith of His people. Make a faith chart with pictures drawn to represent each hero of the faith. Include pictures of your family. Thank God for giving you faith and ask Him to help each family member boldly demonstrate his or her faith as His people did in biblical times.

311

Teach righteousness, discernment, and courage with the stories of ungodly people summarized by Peter (2 Peter 2:1–3:18 RSV). Peter uses familiar stories to remind the people that there always will be false teachers and that we are to become skilled at identifying and avoiding them. Parts of the second chapter may not be understandable for young children, but older children should find them helpful. Note in chapter 3 that Paul gives the people four reminders: "Beloved, be reminded" (vv. 1–2); "Beloved, don't be ignorant" (v. 8); "Beloved, be zealous" (v. 14); and "Beloved, beware" (v. 17).

Have your children write slogans in their own words that correlate with these passages. For example, "Be cool, bro," "Know the truth, dude," "Be a working fool, pal," or "Keep your eyes open, man." Letter the slogans on small signs to post in their rooms as reminders that Jesus will help them stand against friends or acquaintances who try to lead them into un-Christian beliefs or actions.

312

Teach about love with John's word pictures (1 John 2:3–4:21). Give your children a copy of this passage and have them highlight the word *love* each time it occurs. Then read the passage together, stopping to discuss the word love each time you come to it. Ask, "What kind of love does this refer to—romantic love, friendship love, family love, or godly love?" When you read 1 John 3:18, ask, "How will Jesus help us love with deeds and truth?" Have your children make valentines to send to their relatives. It doesn't need to be Valentine's Day to send an "I love you" card.

313

Teach goodness with the stories of Diotrephes and Demetrius (3 John 9–14). Contrast the descriptions of the two men. The information is sketchy but significant. One was a malicious troublemaker, the other an honest encourager of others. Have your children make up a story about these two men, telling some of the things each man might have done to gain his reputation in the early church.

314

Teach courage to stand up for what is right with the story of the message to the church at Laodicea (Revelation 3:14–22). The message to this group was that they were lukewarm. Perhaps they were Christian enough to be accepted by the believers and worldly enough to be accepted by the non-believers. Compare this reference with James 1:6–8, which says that people who allow themselves to go either way in following God are unstable in all areas of their lives. Ask God to forgive you for times when you are a "fence rider" with one foot on both sides of the line. Thank one another for times when you see family members boldly living out their faith in words or actions.

315

Teach the value of being open with God from the Psalms. (For example: Psalm 6, 10, 19, 37, 44.) David was open and honest with God and expressed his concerns, gratitude, fears, and faith. Help each family member start a confidential journal in which they thank God for daily blessings and ask the Lord for help in making difficult decisions.

7 apply values in everyday situations

Philip has been raised in a Christian family. He knows dozens of Bible stories and can quote more than 100 Bible verses. But now that he is away at college and has experienced several confrontations with an atheistic professor, he finds that he is unsure of what he believes about God.

WE ALL HAVE KNOWN families where the parents superimposed values on the children. The children seemed to conform to the values and desires of their parents, but they did so without adopting those values on a personal level.

When our children are young, they readily acknowledge and accept our faith. During adolescence they may question these beliefs. We cannot "believe" our children into heaven. God's Holy Spirit works saving faith in our children. It is our duty to see that their faith is nurtured and strengthened as they study His Word and, when they are old enough, as they celebrate His Meal. Still, don't be alarmed when older children begin to question their faith and yours. Allowing them to discuss issues without suffering negative consequences allows them to work through doubts and to put careful thought into making Christ-like decisions.

Encourage your children to struggle openly with

spiritual doubts and issues. Discuss choices and consequences with them until they can truly accept values such as honesty and kindness as their own. Your children probably will never accept all your values, but they will grow in living out their faith as you let them question and wrestle with the values important to you.

As your children learn what your values are, develop a clear undertanding of what those values mean in terms of attitude and behavior, and watch you model those values as you study God's Word together, they will learn to apply those values in their own lives. This chapter will suggest ways you can help children of all ages notice how other people demonstrate their values, discover how to make godly choices about values, and learn how to understand the consequences of their choices.

Remember Moses' instructions? Parents are to teach their children in the home, when they get up in the morning, when they lie down, and when they walk. The best teaching takes place in everyday situations. Examples are all around you. Use them.

316 Have "pregame huddles." Before going on a family outing, huddle together in the family room and develop a plan for how each person will behave in a way that is consistent with your values. For example, if you are going to the movies, ask your children, "How can we demonstrate courtesy from the time we leave home until we return?" Allow your children to make suggestions. They might think of not fighting over who gets to sit in the front seat, not talking during the movie, or not kicking the seat of the person sitting in front of them. Encourage your children to think of positive behaviors. They can wait patiently in line for popcorn and say thank you when they receive it.

Your goal is not to make the rules but to let your children think of their own ideas. If they need help, you might give a hint or make a suggestion by asking, "How about ...?" As children are encouraged to translate your Christian values into personal behaviors, their understanding of the values increase.

317

Let your children be "Monday morning quarterbacks" and review how successful the family has been in demonstrating values over a given period. While you probably will have a few examples of negative behaviors, focus on reinforcing positive behaviors. Individuals can relate their own experiences as well as those they have observed in other family members. When someone tells about successfully demonstrating a value, cheer for that person, pat him or her on the back, and thank God for helping that individual make a wise choice.

318

When your children tell you about a situation at school where your values are clearly violated, listen carefully. When the story is finished, say, "Rewind. Let's go back to the point where things started to go wrong. Let's restart the story from that point and see if we can write a new ending."

Children may tend to "rewind" to the point when money was stolen, a fight broke out, or graffiti was sprayed across several lockers. Ask them to go further back in the story to see what attitudes and incidents led up to the negative behavior. If you need to help your children understand how to do this, ask, "Why do you think those kids did that? What were they thinking? What values did their behavior reflect? What values of ours did they violate?"

Your goal is to help your children understand that Satan can tempt people to make a series of "small" negative choices that lead to negative attitudes and behaviors. Pray together, asking Jesus to help your child make positive choices that result in positive behaviors.

319

Record television programs to watch together at a later time. When watching the recorded program, use the remote control to pause the tape when a character has to make a decision. Ask your children to identify the decision facing the character, list different choices the character could make, and list the possible results of each choice. Ask your children to identify the best choice the character could make. Then invite them to predict which choice the character will make. Restart the tape and watch to see how the plot unfolds.

You might watch a show in which a man enters his backyard and discovers the neighbor's dog has dug under the fence and scattered trash all over the yard. Then you stop the tape. The options this man has include shooting the dog, calling the dogcatcher, going next door and yelling at the neighbor, requiring the neighbor to clean up the yard, cleaning up the yard himself, helping the neighbor fill in the hole and find ways to strengthen the fence, taking the dog home to the neighbor, laughing at the mess, becoming angry, understanding that the neighbor had nothing to do with the mess, etc. Your goal is to help your children see that there are always choices for behaviors.

When your children become familiar with this activity, let one of them work the remote control and decide when to stop the tape. Always be sure they remember that Jesus stands ready to help them live out their faith and values.

320

When your children share a problem, ask them what choices they can make to handle it. At first they may list only one or two choices, but if you help them think creatively, they may be able to come up with additional choices. Some choices may be ridiculous, but don't discourage your children from brainstorming.

For example, if your child is being hassled on the way to school by an older child, he or she might suggest changing schools or giving the child whatever he or she wants. As you talk, help your child see that there are actually many options to consider: hiring a bodyguard, joining a car pool instead of walking to school, walking with several friends, being kind to the bully by taking him or her cookies, asking you to talk with the other child's parents, or reporting the child to the school authorities. Discuss the appropriateness of different choices and ask God's blessing on the option your child decides to use.

321

Don't rescue your children from the consequences of their choices. Consequences are the best teachers. You can share the consequences with your children, empathize with their feelings, and comfort them, but don't rob them of the learning opportunity.

For example, if your children spend all their allowances early in the week and don't have money to go skating with their friends on Saturday, don't give them an advance on their allowance. Ask, "How can you be sure that next time you will have money to do what you want to do with your friends?" They may suggest giving you the price of admission to hold for them or putting the required amount into an envelope marked with the date and the planned activity. They may ask to receive their allowance Saturday morning rather than Monday morning so they won't spend all their money early in the week. Discussing how to avoid negative consequences gives children hope and a plan.

322

Cut out two large hearts. Draw thrones in the center of each. In one heart write "self" on top of the throne and write "God" in the lower part of the heart. In the other heart write "God" on top of the throne and write "self" in the lower part of the heart. Use the second heart to help children see that when they make choices and do things that are pleasing to God, they honor Him. Then show them the first heart. Explain that when they make choices and do things that are not pleasing to God, they honor themselves. Once they understand what the hearts mean, you can use them to help you discuss making appropriate decisions.

323 Buy or make a family bulletin board. Choose a regular night each week for the family to share incidents in which they have lived out their Christian values. Affirm one another. Then have each person make a decoration for the bulletin board that represents the incident they shared. Post these until the next week when they will be replaced. Use the bulletin board as a prayer reminder, thanking God for helping you live out your faith and asking for His guidance in making difficult decisions. Keep the decorations in your family values scrapbook for future reference and remembering.

324 Invite your children to voice their doubts or disagreements about certain values you want to teach them. Listen carefully to what they are saying— Satan can use those doubts to keep your children from owning godly values. Take the time to fully discuss, explore, and pray about their doubts. Find ways to answer as many of the doubts as possible.

For example, your teenagers might not agree with your value of chastity. Their arguments might be that most of their friends are sexually active; they can practice contraception to avoid pregnancy or disease; they plan to marry their dating partner some day; they don't plan on marrying until they graduate from college and become established in a career and they don't want to wait that long to have sex; they will be rejected by their friends; their dating partner will break up with them unless they have sex; their sexually active friends don't seem to experience negative consequences; etc.

Direct commands such as "Do it because I say so" or "Do it because the Bible says so" won't have much impact on the choices your teenagers will make about chastity and other issues. Discuss the reasons they give you, don't just negate them. These thoughts and doubts are the obstacles you face when trying to teach your children your values. You will find good information to help you and your teenager sift through issues important to them in *Why Wait?* by Josh McDowell and Dick Day (Here's Life Press, 1987) and *Steer Clear: A Christian Guide to Teen Temptations* by Kathleen Winkler (Concordia, 1997).

325

Work together to draw a flow chart of a situation (real or fictional) that shows the progression of events and the different decisions made. Use rectangles for actions, diamonds for decisions, and circles for thoughts. This is an excellent way to help your children see how behaviors lead to thoughts, which lead to decisions, which result in behaviors, etc.

326

Have your children retell one of their favorite stories. Identify the values demonstrated by the characters in the story. Then assign a different set of values to each character and see how they behave differently and how the story outcome is affected.

For example, you might use the story of Goldilocks and the three bears. Goldilocks did not respect the bears' privacy. She selfishly stole their food, broke their chairs, and went to sleep in one of their beds. What if Goldilocks were kind, giving, and helpful? Might she have prepared food for the bears? Might she have cleaned their house? Would she have waited outside until the bears came home?

327

Many values you want to teach your children will need to be modeled. Try using an "on the job" training system to teach these behaviors and values. This technique has six steps.

- Describe the behavior.

- Demonstrate the behavior while describing it.

- Ask your children to act out the behavior as you describe each step.

- Ask your children to do the behavior while describing it themselves.

- Give your children opportunities to practice the behavior.

- Help your children evaluate how well they can do the behavior.

This technique is helpful for teaching table manners and skills such as doing the laundry, cooking, driving, building things, or sewing. It also helps teach skills such as how to confront a friend who is tempting one to disobey or how to make a Christian witness to a friend who needs help. Behaviors such as these will strengthen values such as industry, self-reliance, helpfulness, and courtesy.

328 Establish appropriate rewards for positive behaviors as well as consequences for negative behaviors. List the behaviors that demonstrate your values, then work together to decide on rewards for making positive choices. Be just as consistent in applying the positive consequences as you are in applying the negative consequences. Remind your children that we live out our faith as a loving reaction to what God has done for us in Jesus. Rewards can include saying the child's name in a thank-You prayer, allowing the child to make more of his or her own decisions, etc.

329 Have your children try to list their daily behaviors that are not related to values. Then discuss the list, eliminating any behaviors to which you can attach a value. The final list should be quite short because almost all our behaviors have some relationship to values.

For example, one child might add eating to the list. During the discussion you might decide that courtesy is involved in eating (making sure everyone has been passed food) as is patience (waiting until mealtime to eat), courage (trying new foods), self-control (not eating dessert first), and self-reliance (preparing one's own meal).

330 Support your children. When they fail to make a wise decision and are upset with themselves because of the outcome, discuss the whole situation. Then affirm them with a sincere, "I believe in you. Jesus will help you do better next time."

331 Give your children opportunities to contribute to the family. Even young children can help with chores. Don't undermine their sense of accomplishment or confidence by criticizing how they did their work or redoing what they did. Remaking the bed or resetting the table will give children the message that their contribution was rejected. They are devalued. The first time you assign a chore, work beside your child, saying, "Let me show you how to do this." Praise your child's efforts and say thanks often. Praise them for ingenuity in completing the task differently from your normal way of doing things.

332 Teach your children the joy of giving to others. Encourage them to give things they have made— pictures, cards, bouquets, cookies, decorated pillows, framed photographs, painted ceramic figurines, etc.—to family members or friends. Affirm their generosity and let them know how thrilled you are when they do nice things for others. You might want to do a servant project together, perhaps baking cookies and making small gifts for homebound members of your church.

333 Build a faith memorial from rocks like the Israelites used to do. Collect several small rocks and wash them. Label each rock with words that will recall an incident in which your family's faith in God was strengthened. These incidents might include answered prayers, having an accident without serious injury, receipt of unexpected money just when an emergency bill needed to be paid, or a child's saying no to an offer of drugs. Retell the stories as you work on the project. Add the date of the incident to each rock. Then arrange the rocks in an appropriate container and set it by the fireplace or in the family room. Whenever a new incident occurs, record it on a new rock and add it to the memorial.

334

Make a faith scrapbook. Fill it with stories and photographs you take at times when your family experiences a faith crisis or a faith blessing from God.

335

Cut out a copy of an "Ann Landers" or "Dear Abby" column from the newspaper. Read one of the letters and the columnist's response. Ask, "What values are involved in this letter? What values are indicated in the response? How would we answer this question differently?"

336

Start a storybook about a family just like yours, but give the characters different names. Every week choose one incident from your experiences that would make a good story for the book. Work together to write a parallel story to the incident. Describe how characters arrived at certain decisions and how their values influenced them. This book will make great reading as your children grow older. It also will help them evaluate choices they have made and see how they have grown in their faith.

337

Make a "Best Decision" chart. Each day every family member writes the most significant decision he or she made that day on a self-adhesive note, signs his or her name, and sticks the note to the chart. Once a week take time to read aloud each decision as you remove them to make room for the next week's notes. Give one another encouragement and affirmation for having demonstrated Christian values through wise decision making. Thank God for helping you live out your faith in everyday tasks.

338

Use a large shoe box to make a "How to Make Wise Decisions" kit. Have your children suggest what might go into the kit. You might include a pencil and paper for listing pros and cons, a Bible, a picture of Jesus, a list of your top-priority values, and a construction paper heart with "love" written on it.

Explain that your children won't carry the kit with them, but when they are faced with a decision, they can think about the kit and find ways to use similar resources to help them make wise choices. Memorizing Scripture ensures that children will have God's guidance with them at all times. Older children and adults can find a pencil and paper wherever they are. Children can pray, asking God what He would have them do. The actual kit is a visual aid to help family members remember the resources available to them.

339

Become "Graffiti Busters." Purchase neutral paint (for example, gray or tan) and some paintbrushes.

When you see graffiti on a fence or a wall, talk to the owner and offer to paint over it. (Some home-owners may have leftover paint you could use.) Make sure to get appropriate permission before painting government property—signs, utility boxes, etc.

340

Visit the zoo. Ask your children to see if they notice any behaviors exhibited by the animals that would reflect values. They might notice a mother loving her baby or a small animal acting courageous. But they won't see much honesty, sharing, generosity, or thrift. Explain that God created human beings in His image. Animals act on instinct. We can think about how we will act, depending on God to guide us and to forgive us when we fail.

341

Participate in a project to clean up the community or protect the environment. Read Genesis 1:28–31 and explain that God gave us the responsibility to care for the earth. Explain how the project you are working on is one way of taking care of God's cre-ation.

342

Attend your children's sports activities. Watch for things during the games that suggest your values. After the game ask your children which values are important to practice when playing a team sport. Share the things you noticed. If your children are having difficulty making the connection, ask, "What if someone were dishonest in claiming they were not out of bounds?" Or ask, "What if someone said one of the other team members fouled him or her but it wasn't true?" Sports also provide excellent opportunities to teach teamwork.

343 Play a harmonic chord on the piano and ask your children how it sounds. Then change one note so the chord sounds terrible. Ask your children how it sounds. Explain that when they behave in harmony with Christian values, their behavior is pleasing to God and to others. When they behave in ways that clash with Christian values, their behavior is displeasing to God and to others. Ask, "How can we live in harmony with Christian values? How do we live in disharmony?"

344 Encourage your children to learn to play a musical instrument. This helps them develop self-discipline and self-confidence.

345 Read 1 Corinthians 6:19–20, which says that our bodies are the temples of the Holy Spirit. Have your children discuss how they should care for the house of God. Some ideas might include refusing to allow inappropriate mental input, controlling one's thoughts, eating properly, exercising, not going to inappropriate places, not taking drugs, not becoming sexually active before marriage, filling the mind with Scripture, going to places that please God, and making sure our words and actions are in line with appropriate values.

346

Rather than having a garage sale or making a donation to a thrift shop, use your children's outgrown clothes and toys to teach generosity and kindness. Make sure the clothes are clean and mended and that the toys still work. Then take your children to a local orphanage or shelter for the homeless to deliver the clothes and toys.

347

Have your children try an experiment. Go to a place with a lot of people, perhaps a supermarket or a mall. While they walk along, have your children make a face that suggests they are angry. Ask them to observe how people respond. Some adults may look startled, frown, turn away, or even make a critical comment. Then have your children put on a happy face as they walk along. Ask them to look people straight in the eye and watch for responses. Most people will respond with a matching smile.

When discussing the experiment, point out that frowns usually create more frowns and smiles usually create more smiles. The same is true of appropriate behavior. When we choose to act on our values, we encourage others to do the same. (Be sure to remind your children never to approach a stranger—even one who is smiling. This experiment should be conducted only in your presence.)

348

Encourage children to put themselves in the role of the main character in a story or on a television program. Ask, "What would you have done in that situation? How would knowing about Jesus' love help you solve that problem?"

349

Buy a pet for your children. Caring for a pet can teach children how to be gentle, loving, dependable, disciplined, and kind. Discuss how a pet depends on its owners and needs to be able to count on them. List things your children will do to care for the animal, and affirm them when they are faithful in doing these things. Discuss these things with your children before buying the pet to determine if they are willing to commit their time to giving it proper care.

350

Give your children opportunities to practice patience. When you and your children are stuck in a long line, ask them what they could do to make patient waiting easier. Make homemade cinnamon rolls, letting them rise two or three times. Explain that even though you have to wait a long time for the dough to rise properly, it makes the rolls light, fluffy, and tasty. Talk about a time when you have prayed to God and patiently waited for His guidance.

351

Watch for what each child does when he or she quietly entertains himself or herself. Your children may enjoy reading, doing crossword puzzles, building things, or playing with a toy. This will give you a clue for items to have in the car for your children when there is an unexpected wait. If you don't have books or toys with you, a distraction can help children learn to wait patiently. You always can play "I see something blue." Your children try to guess what it is. All questions must be phrased so you can answer with only a yes or a no. The person correctly identifying the object gets to start the game over again.

352

Take older children to court to observe a trial. Discuss what values the defendant is accused of violating. Discuss what justice means and what might be the just consequence for the defendant if he or she is found guilty. Help your children understand that issues of justice occur in everyday life.

353

When one of your children offends another (verbally, physically, or by taking something without permission), use the opportunity to talk about justice and mercy. Justice would require that the offender be punished while mercy could mean acknowledging the wrongdoing and not punishing the offender. Encourage the offended child to practice mercy in this situation. Thank God for the mercy He shows in not counting our sins against us.

354

Use a dandelion to help children learn how to be gentle. Explain that a dandelion is so fragile that you can break it apart simply by blowing on it. Have them practice touching the seed pod so gently that it does not break apart. Then explain that people are fragile in many ways and that they must learn to treat others gently. They can practice being gentle with their pets, toys, and books. Let them hold one of your precious figurines after extracting a promise that they will be very gentle with it.

355

Gather a load of white rags and include one red rag that is not colorfast. Show your children the rags and tell them that the white rags represent a group of friends who all agree on Christian values. The red rag represents a friend or acquaintance who holds some wrong beliefs. Put all the rags in the washing machine and run them through a cycle using hot water.

While the load is washing, talk about how friends can influence one another. Say, "You may think it won't make any difference if you hang around people whose values you don't agree with, but what you may not know is that some of that person's beliefs may begin to affect yours." When the wash is through, let your children see how all the white rags have taken on some of the red color from the red rag. Encourage your children to gather friends around them whose values are similar to your own.

356

Teach your children how to maintain long-distance friendships. Encourage them to make short telephone calls, write letters, send cards and e-mail messages, remember birthdays with gifts, and send copies of school photographs. Read Proverbs 18:24 and discuss ways to be a good friend.

357 When children argue, you have an opportunity to help them work on peacemaking. You may have a better chance at getting through to your children if you wait until tempers have calmed down. But using an actual situation as a point of discussion will help your children relate to what you are saying.

Ask your children if they remember the argument (and other similar arguments). Ask them if arguing ever solves a disagreement. They probably will say no. Ask what kinds of things do solve arguments. Help them understand the concepts of accommodation, compromise, taking turns, forgiveness, and agreeing to disagree.

358 Explain loyalty to your children by pointing out how loyal they are to a favorite sports team. Ask, "Are they still your favorite team when they lose?" Children will probably answer that they are. Explain that this demonstrates their loyalty to that team. Ask, "What would make you change your mind about the team and pick another team to be your favorite?" If they assert that nothing would do that, say admiringly, "You are truly loyal, aren't you?" Help children brainstorm ways in which they can demonstrate loyalty to their family, church, school, and friends.

359

Whenever you hear your children putting themselves down, point out that they are being disrespectful to themselves. Saying things such as "I'm so stupid," "I can't do anything right," or "I am clumsy" is negative self-talk. Ask your children how they would feel if a best friend said those things about them. They probably would be upset. Yet people often talk to themselves in very destructive ways. Encourage your children to develop positive self-talk. Examples might include "I'll do better next time." "Jesus will help me do this." "I can figure this out."

Be careful never to put a child down in anger. Ask your child's forgiveness if you do. Helping develop the habit of positive self-talk celebrates the redemption Jesus has won for your child.

360

When your children become emotional as they tell you about something that happened to a friend, they are demonstrating sensitivity and empathy. Don't miss the opportunity to affirm these qualities in your children. Say, "I am so pleased to see that you are so sensitive to how your friend is feeling. That's a terrific quality you have."

361

Surround your children with people whose values are most like your own. In other words be sure your friends are those who will have a positive influence on both you and your children. Invite people to your home who exemplify values with which you agree. Spend an evening discussing how their values have influenced their lives.

362

Give your children a list of your top-priority values and a list of their opposites. Have them watch a favorite cartoon show and circle in red those values illustrated in the cartoon. Then have them watch an episode of a show developed to teach children appropriate values. This time draw blue circles around the values. Compare and contrast the results and discuss what each show is teaching.

363

Obtain a biography of one of your children's positive role models and read it aloud with them. Have your children keep track of the values demonstrated in the biography and how they have influenced the person's life. Ask your children if they think the person is a Christian. How do the person's actions demonstrate faith in Christ or the lack of it?

364

Take your children to an art museum. Give each child a sheet of paper with your top-priority values listed. Challenge your children to find as many of these values illustrated in the paintings as they can. When they find one, your children should point out the picture and explain the value illustrated.

365

Teach your children to show respect for the neighborhood by asking them to help you maintain an attractive yard, neatly mowed and trimmed, and a clutter-free driveway.

366

Help your children design and distribute flyers to everyone on your street that invite them to a free car wash at your house. (No donations accepted.) Have fun washing cars and show your children that helping your neighbors can be a great experience.

367

Make up care packages for homeless individuals. Include such things as combs; small soaps; shampoo; matches; candles; instant coffee; packets of sugar, salt, and pepper; packages of instant soup; tea bags; a mug; and other items that might be welcomed. Include a card or note that witnesses your faith in Jesus. Take the packages to an organization in your town that distributes to the homeless.

368

Take turns giving one another foot massages. Talk about how good it feels when someone rubs your feet. Compare this experience to Jesus washing the disciples' feet. Discuss how it feels to be a servant and to do something that makes someone else feel good. Ask your children to list other things they might do to make others feel good. Suggest that they try doing one of these things the next day and report back on what happened and how it made them feel.

369

On slips of paper, write incomplete sentences that name differing values. You might include "I am kind when I ...," "I am honest when I ...," and similar phrases. Have family members take turns drawing a slip, reading the sentence, and filling in the ending.

370

Take up a new family sport such as skiing. Talk about how the sport challenges you to be courageous when you look down a slope. Share in reasonable risk taking. Laugh at the failures and falls. Enjoy the thrill of success. Make each ski trip memorable in a pleasant way.

371

Read your children a book about individuals who have suffered for what they believed. A history of Washington's men at Valley Forge or a biography of Dr. Martin Luther King Jr. are examples. Let your children imagine how the soldiers lived through the winter with little food and few clothes or how Dr. King suffered through violence and imprisonment. Ask, "What would make someone go through that? What values were being fought for? What would be so important that someone would voluntarily endure those conditions?"

Ask your children which of their values are so strong that they would be willing to suffer discomfort to remain true to them. Remind them of the value with which Jesus blesses us in His willingness to give His life for us.

372

Take your children to see a copy of the Declaration of Independence. Have one child read it aloud. Ask everyone to identify what values caused the founders of our country to write this document.

373 Turn off all the lights in the house and darken the family room by covering any windows. Have one child light a candle. Tell your children that sharing Jesus' love is like lighting a candle in a dark room. People notice the light and are glad to see it. And the light of even a little candle can be seen from a long distance.

374 Take your children to a park with a pond or a lake. Toss a small stone into the water. Ask them to notice how the circles form around the point of the stone's impact and expand over the water's surface. Explain that our behaviors can have a similar effect. One action can have several consequences and affect a lot of other people. Give examples from your own life. Ask your children to think of examples of how they were affected by the actions of others. Ask Jesus' help in living out Christian values that will have a positive influence on others rather than a negative one.

375 Have your children bake two cakes from scratch. Carefully follow the recipe in making the first cake. Omit baking powder or soda and eggs in the second cake. While the cakes are baking, talk about how mixing all the ingredients and baking them together makes a perfect dessert. Point out that the different ingredients blend together and can't be isolated once the cake is finished. When the cakes are done, compare the two. The one with the missing ingredients should be much flatter and not taste as good.

Share that this experiment illustrates why it is important to ask God to help us develop a set of positive values. Through the redemptive work of His Son, God has "baked" into us Christian values. He has made us pleasing to Himself and someone whom people will want to befriend. When we fail to live out our Christian values, the resulting behaviors often cause others to reject us in much the same way as the cake missing the ingredients was rejected.

376

Have one family member use your computer to start writing about a value important to you. Keep the disk next to the computer and encourage other family members to add to what was written until you have several pages on that value. Print a copy and read it as a family. Put it in your family values scrapbook. Then start a second document about a different value. Do this until you have written about each of your top-priority values.

377

Read some of Patrick Henry's speeches to your children and discuss how the speeches illustrate his values. Do this with other historical and biblical figures.

378

Read historical accounts of social injustices: slavery, taking land from Native Americans, apartheid in South Africa, or the Holocaust. Discuss how wrong values were demonstrated and resulted in negative consequences for everyone involved. Talk about ways your family can fight against social injustice in your community.

379

Invite a missionary home on furlough to stay at your home for a week or two. Invite him or her to tell about sharing the Gospel with people in another land, the living conditions, the difficulties, and the rewards. Have him or her share how his or her values are demonstrated by actions. Let this person be one more guide for your children, pointing them toward their Savior and the development of positive values.

380

Make your home a safe place for children to visit. Treat your children's friends with the same respect you would give to one of your adult friends. Make children feel welcome. Provide treats. Suggest games they can play. Include visitors in your values-teaching activities. When discussing values and other related topics, it is helpful for your children to hear the ideas of other kids their own age. It also will help you know what values your children's friends have and notice how these may influence your own children's choices.

381

With your children, list several opposites to the values you hold dear. Then brainstorm all the reasons to reject each negative value. This activity helps your children to develop a resistance to harmful values and a reluctance to go along with them.

8 reinforce values through games

> *Betty looked out the kitchen window and watched her 10-year-old twins building a clubhouse. They had been working hard for several hours. It was almost finished. "If I worked them that hard around the house, they would say I was being cruel," she said aloud in the empty room. "But as long as they call it play, they'll work all day."*

THAT'S RIGHT, BETTY. Children love to play. And playing is one way that children learn about many things.

> *Eight-year-old Jimmy used to have problems with math, but after his mom taught him several card games that required him to add and multiply his points, his math scores improved. Six-year-old Cindy learned about taking turns and patiently waiting her turn by playing simple board games with her family. Joe learned what it meant to be a good sport by playing Little League baseball. Sharon learned how to bake a cake using her play stove that actually baked little cakes in tiny pans.*

Many "games" take as much effort as productive

work, but children view play as fun. Take advantage of your children's natural affinity for play and reinforce the values you are teaching through games. Here are a few suggestions.

382

Design a crossword puzzle using the values highly important to you. Number the boxes appropriately and write clues. Give copies of the puzzle to your children and see who can get the most correct responses. A variation of this game would be to challenge older children to develop a puzzle for younger siblings or for you to work.

383

Design a word search that incorporates the names of your top-priority values. Place the value words in a straight or diagonal line. Give your children a list of the values you have built into the word search and see who can find all the words first.

384

Play "I Spy." Give your children a list of your top-priority values, then watch a television show together. Whenever a child sees a behavior that demonstrates a value on the list, he or she calls out "I spy" and identifies the behavior. The other children try to guess which value is being attached to the behavior. If this game is too disruptive during a favorite family show, use a prerecorded video.

385

Give each child a slip of paper with a situation and a value that situation implies written on it. Then have your children take turns miming the situation, playing all the parts involved. Other family members try to guess what situation and value is being communicated.

386

Make your own version of "Old Maid" by using cards on which you have written the names of your values. You will need to make two cards for each virtue and one "old maid" card, which has a negative value on it such as "Disloyalty." Play the game using the rules for "Old Maid."

387

Buy or borrow a copy of a game called "The Ungame." It is a family communication board game in which you are periodically directed to draw a card and respond to the question or instructions on the card. Write a series of cards for a values version and play the game using your new cards. Here are some sample cards: "Tell about the last time you were totally honest." "Tell about a time when someone acted lovingly toward you." "What does *courage* mean to you?" "Describe an act of loyalty." "Describe an act of kindness."

388

Give your children a list of Scripture verses (from some of the activities in chapter 1) that address Christian values. Have each child use his or her own Bible to look up the verses and identify the value. Set a timer and see who finishes first with the most correct responses. If you wish, stagger start times so older children start a few minutes after younger ones.

389

Buy or borrow a game called "Bible Treasure Trails" published by the Bible Memory Association. This teaching game awards extra points to players who can say the Scripture verse from memory. Make additional Bible verse cards using verses that emphasize your values. Use these cards instead of the ones that come with the game.

390

Make a scorecard that lists your children's names down the left side and values you wish to reinforce across the top. Go to a basketball court and take turns shooting baskets. The first basket each person shoots determines if they get two points under the first value. The second shot is for the second value and soon. Keep going back to the first value and working through them all until someone wins by having two points under each value.

391

Borrow several instant-print cameras. Give your children a list of values and send them on a scavenger hunt to find examples of those values. They can photograph people acting in ways consistent with the values or signs that use a value word. Assign a time for your children to return to the house. Have snacks waiting. Have each child explain what he or she found and show the pictures. If using cameras isn't feasible, children can list what they found.

392 Play Pictionary using phrases you have written in advance. The phrases should relate to your top-priority values. Divide your family into two teams. The teams take turns trying to communicate phrases by drawing symbols and pictures on a large flip chart. No words or letters can be used, but any drawing is acceptable.

393 Cover a page with rows of dots which, when connected, would form small squares. In the center of each square, write the first letter of one of your top-priority values. Then give one sheet to each two family members. Players draw one line between two dots for each turn. When a player draws a line that completes a square, he or she initials the square and gets to draw one more line. The game is over when all the dots are connected and all the squares completed. Count up the number of squares each person initialed to see who won. Then have players count up the different values listed in their squares and see who gets the highest number.

394 Print the names of values important to you on index cards. Attach yarn so family members can wear the cards around their necks. Divide the family into two teams. Instruct one team to hold hands and stand at one end of the yard. The other team holds hands and faces the first team, leaving about 15 yards between the teams. Play "Red Rover" by calling out the value an individual is wearing. For example, "Red Rover, Red Rover, let *honesty* come over." Then the family member with the honesty name tag runs and tries to break through the other team's line by pushing against the clasped hands. If the individual breaks through, the family member returns to his or her team, taking along one of the players whose clasp was broken. If the line does not break, the individual joins the other team. The game ends when only one person is left on one of the teams. Note: You may need to recruit some neighbors to play this game.

395

Write the names of values on slips of paper and tape the slips to pieces of hard, wrapped candy. Hide these candies around the house and give your children 20 minutes to see how many they can find. (Be sure to retrieve any pieces of candy the children didn't find so the ants won't find them later.)

396

Cut out small cardboard shapes (star, square, triangle, circle, etc.) and write the names of different values on each one. Arrange the shapes on a cookie sheet and play a memory game. Have your children study the shapes for 30 to 60 seconds, then close their eyes. Remove one shape, then tell your children to open their eyes. They have to guess what shape and what value you removed. When someone guesses correctly, show the shape and return it to the cookie sheet. Whoever guesses correctly gets to be the next person to remove a shape while the rest of you close your eyes.

397 Play "Hangman" using the names of your top-priority values.

398 Play "Mother, May I?" with a twist. Children stand several yards away from you. You call out to one child, "Take two giant (or baby or scissors or backward) steps." The child then asks, "Mother, may I?" Your response would be "You may if you are honest (or another value)." The child says, "I am honest," and takes the steps. If the child fails to ask permission, he or she must return to the starting point. The goal is to be the first child to reach you.

399 Play a trust game by dividing family members into teams of two persons each. One partner is blindfolded and the other partner leads him or her around, calling out instructions such as: "Duck down so you won't hit your head." "Step a little to the right." "Step up." "We're going downhill." The guide should lead the person along a safe path but give the impression that there are dangers on every side. After the experience, talk about trust and why it is sometimes hard to trust someone. Ask, "Why do we know we always can trust God to care for us?"

400 Make a deck of cards by writing values you wish to reinforce on poster board rectangles. Make an even number of cards for each value. Use the deck to play "Go Fish."

401 Play "20 Questions" with the names of values. Think of one value you are teaching your children and announce, "I've got a value in mind." Your children ask 20 questions that can be answered yes or no. Whoever guesses the correct value takes the next turn.

402 Go to your local Christian bookstore and look for games that teach values. Purchase one and play it with your children.

403 Write the names of values on small white buttons. Then play "Button, Button, Who's Got the Button?" with young children. In this version, take one of the buttons and say the name of the value, for example, "Faith, Faith, who's got the faith?"

404 Make a home version of Wheel of Fortune by creating a dial with dollar amounts on each segment. Write several short phrases about values to use as puzzles. On a blank sheet of paper draw the correct number of squares for the letters in a phrase. Leave spaces between words. Players take turns spinning the dial and calling out letters. If they guess correctly, they add the dollar amount to their score. You act as Vanna White and write letters in the appropriate squares when they are correctly guessed. The goal is to solve the puzzles and to win the most "money."

405 Play a home version of Jeopardy using values. Make up at least nine squares with answers on them relating to values. The correct question for each answer should be "What is (name of a value)? Turn the cards upside down and write point values on the backs. Arrange the cards on a table. Your children take turns turning over a card, reading the answer aloud, then posing the corresponding question. If they give the correct question, they take the square and accumulate the points on the back of the card. The object is to win as many points as possible.

406 Play a home version of Concentration using values. Draw a rebus for the puzzle the players must solve. Then cover the surface of the rebus with small cards. Written on these cards are the names of values you want to reinforce. Place the cards values side down. Make two cards for each value. Players then take turns turning over two cards. If the cards match, they are removed, a portion of the rebus is exposed, and the player gets another turn. If the cards do not match, both are turned back down and the next player takes a turn. The first person to solve the rebus under the puzzle wins the game.

407 List your top-priority values, then scramble the letters in each word. Challenge your children to unscramble the words. The first person to decode all the words correctly wins. For older children, include a scrambled definition for each value.

408

Play "Pickup Sticks" but assign values to the different colors. For example, red sticks might be honesty, blue sticks might be loyalty, yellow sticks might be self-control. Keep track of who gets the most sticks for each value.

409

Play "Simon Says" using your values as adjectives. This allows your children to have fun with the names of the values. For example: "Simon says, 'Take two honest steps.' " "Simon says, 'With great self-control, hop three times.' " "Simon says, 'Jump up in the air with courage.' " Of course, if children do something that you did not preface with "Simon says," they are eliminated from the game.

410

Give your children coloring books and color together. As you color, ask your children to make up stories about the characters. Ask: "Do you think this little girl is honest? How would she exercise self-control? What might she do to show that she is courageous?"

411

Go to the beach and have a sand castle competition. Name each castle for a different member of the "Royal Family of Values," for example, the King of Courage, the Queen of Honesty, the Duke of Self-Control, the Princess of Loyalty, the Duchess of Love, or the Prince of Respect. Make flags for each castle using triangles of construction paper and toothpicks. Print the names of the residents of the castles on the flags. As they build the castles, ask your children to take turns describing their royal family member and how his or her life demonstrates the name.

412 Set up a matching game. In one column list the names of values you want to reinforce. In a second column give brief definitions of each value. Mix the list so the definitions are not directly across from the values they match. Give copies of the list to your children and see who can correctly match the values to their definitions.

413 Play "Tiddly Winks" with values. Label the inner circle of the target as "heart," the next circle as "actions," and the largest circle as "mind." Label the small disks with the names of values. Players take turns aiming the small circles at the target. Players get 10 points for getting a value in the heart, six points for getting a value in the actions, and five points for getting a value in the mind. The player with the highest points for a particular value wins for that value. (There can be a separate winner for each value.)

414 Give your children a Mr. Potato Head. Have them take turns making different characters with the parts provided. Each time they begin a new face, change the assignment. Say, "This time make a Mr. Potato Head who looks honest." "How would he look if you could trust him?" See if your children can make different looks to demonstrate different values. Talk about how people perceive us as we live out different values with our words and actions.

415

Play Dominoes with cardboard dominoes you made using the names of 12 values. Play the game by matching values instead of numbers.

416

Play Scrabble using only words that name values or that are related to values. If this is too difficult for younger children, play regular Scrabble but give a quadruple score for any value name played.

417

Play "Name That Tune" with songs that include or describe your top-priority values. For example, use "Jesus Loves Me," "I Am Trusting Thee, Lord Jesus," "I've Got the Joy," etc. See how many songs your children can recognize. Rather than two people competing for how few notes it will take them to name a tune, let everyone participate. Play or sing the first few notes of a song and see if anyone recognizes it. If not, start over and play a longer section. Keep doing this until someone can name the song. Award extra points for being able to identify the value referred to in the song.

418

Write the names of values on index cards. Under the value name give three definitions, one correct definition and two that are false. Play "Call My Bluff." Two family members are the competitors with three other individuals forming a panel. The first panelist announces a value and reads one definition then passes the card to the next panelist. This panelist reads a second definition and passes the card to the last panelist, who reads the third definition. The two competitors guess which person gave the correct definition. Award five points for a correct guess. See which competitor can earn the most points.

419

Help your children learn about self-control by listing situations that would offer an opportunity to exercise self-control. Call out the different situations one at a time and have your children tell how the situation would call for self-control. Examples might include eating, working, skiing, dieting, exercising, talking, listening, or feeling angry.

420

Make situation cards by describing incidents that illustrate dependability and undependability. Shuffle the cards. Draw one card and read it to your children. Have them identify whether the person in the situation is dependable or undependable and why. Situational examples might include when a friends fails to meet you at the park as promised, when the school bus driver stops at your house every day at 7:30 A.M., when a child at school steals your book, when Dad goes to work every day, or when God keeps you safe every day.

reward success

"*I was looking around my office the other day and I noticed how many mementos reminded me of times I have been rewarded at work,*" John told his wife one evening. "*There were plaques for a couple of special projects I had worked on, a certificate for perfect attendance for the last five years, a little trophy our department received for exceeding performance quotas, and a photograph of the president of the company shaking hands with me at the annual employee awards dinner. Even my large corner office was a reward for hard work that qualified me for my promotion!*"

"*You're right,*" Evelyn replied. "*My company does a lot of employee recognition too. It helps people feel appreciated and needed.*"

"*I was thinking that we haven't been doing enough of that at home. We need to plan ways to recognize the kids when they do things we want them to do. You know, like when we see signs that they are acting on the values we try so hard to teach them.*"

"*I see what you mean,*" Evelyn said thoughtfully. "*There are a lot of things we could do. It would be fun!*"

"*And worthwhile,*" John replied.

JOHN AND EVELYN have the right idea. Recognition and rewards reinforce behaviors. When a behavior is followed by positive reinforcement, that behavior is likely to be repeated. We all like to be recognized and rewarded. So don't miss out on opportunities to do this for your children as part of your teaching process. Too many parents specialize in catching children doing something wrong. Instead, become a parent who specializes in catching them doing something right. Rather than giving your children the idea that they are "earning" your love or God's favor, try ideas such as these.

421

Develop a special notebook for each child. Each time your child demonstrates a value you are reinforcing, make an entry in the notebook. You might write, "Today Sean shared Jesus' love by helping his little sister make her bed. He showed patience, gentleness, and responsibility." You may include snapshots, narrative accounts, or "congratulations" cards you send to celebrate the growth. This is like a grown-up "baby book."

422

Prepare a special dinner in honor of your child who recently has demonstrated ownership of a value through behaviors or words. Prepare his or her favorite foods—even if they don't seem to go together! Pray together, thanking God for helping your child live out the value.

423 Make a unique dessert to show your appreciation for how well your children are learning your values. Consider cherries jubilee, baked Alaska, home-made cream puffs, or make-your-own sundaes. Serve the dessert with lots of praise and affirmation for each individual family member.

424 Designate a wall in the home to be a "Family Hall of Fame." When your children demonstrate your values in a particularly noteworthy way, commemorate the incident on the wall. You might take a picture and enlarge it. Write across the lower portion of the photograph an affirming message, "Congratulations, Eric, Jesus helped you act unselfishly today," and add the date. Or you might write a narrative account of the incident and frame it. You might even have a plaque made at a trophy shop. When you add a new commemoration to the wall, have a family celebration and thank God for helping your child live out the value.

425 Make a special flower arrangement for your child as a reward. Put it in his or her room with a congratulatory card to let the recipient know how much it means to you when your child lives out Christian values. If your child would appreciate it, you might make the arrangement from silk flowers so it would last for a long time.

426 Make coupons that can be redeemed on demand. Give one of these to your children when they deserve recognition. The coupons can be for any-thing that might be meaningful to your children. For example: "This coupon is good for staying up one extra hour on a Friday night." "This coupon is good for a hamburger at _____." "This coupon is good for a 15-minute back rub." "This coupon is good for my reading a story to you." "This coupon is good for my playing a game of your choice with you."

Use both the giving of the coupon and your child's redemption of the coupon as reminders to pray together, asking God's Holy Spirit to continue to strengthen you and your child as you live out your faith.

427

Include stories of your children's success in living out your values in a family newsletter. Send it to rel-atives and close friends several times a year, not just at Christmas. Give your children copies of the newsletters so they can add them to their personal values notebooks.

428

Sometimes your children will do something truly noteworthy that demonstrates your values. When this happens, memorialize it by writing the story and submitting it to an appropriate Christian magazine or your local newspaper. If it is printed, put a copy in your child's notebook. If professional publication isn't possible, develop your own family periodical describing the event.

429 Hug your child. Give a warm "bear hug," holding your child close to you for at least a full minute. This means more than a quick squeeze. Tell your child, "Jesus loves you and so do I."

430 Give your child a back rub or a neck rub. For a back rub, warm a bottle of lotion in a bowl of hot water. Pour a generous amount of lotion on your hands and begin rubbing with long strokes, starting with both hands next to the spine at the bottom of the back. Move up to the neck, then out toward the shoulders, and down the sides of the back. Using a circular motion is very soothing. See how many incidents you can remember when Jesus used physical touch—blessing the little children, taking Jairus' daughter by the hand—as you work.

431 Give your child a foot rub. Have your child soak his or her feet in warm soapy water for several minutes before the massage. Dry the feet. Using warm lotion, massage the bottoms of the feet and the area between the toes. Talk about how the massage reminds you of Jesus washing His disciples' feet.

432 Put your arm around your child. This gesture communicates camaraderie, partnership, caring, and acceptance.

433 Give your child a big smile. Smile not only with your mouth, but with your eyes. And look your child in the eye when you smile and talk together.

434 Prepare a bubble bath for your child. You might put a portable compact disc player in the room to play your child's favorite music.

435 Cuddle with your young child. On a cold or rainy evening build a fire in the fireplace and cover up with a warm blanket. The warmth communicates a sense of well-being and pleasure. Talk about how Jesus holds you safely in His arms.

436 Brush your little girl's hair while telling her how much you love her.

437 Plan extra time to be with your child. Often our time is the one thing we don't think we can afford to give our children. But if we look at things from an eternal perspective, we would agree that affirming our children is more important than doing the dishes immediately after dinner. Let the dishes soak in hot water until your children are asleep. Young children develop loving images of God through the actions of their parents.

438 Let your child plan special activities for an entire weekend. As you spend time with your child in favorite activities, tell him or her the many ways he or she is a blessing to you. Let your child hear you pray, thanking God for His gift of this child to you.

439 Say, "I am very pleased at what you did, but I am not surprised. Jesus is helping you become good at this." When your children know that you believe in them, your faith gives them strength.

440 Share how your child's success makes you feel. Say, "I am so excited (happy, joyous, thrilled, pleased) because of what you did. Your loving action blessed me too." A parent's approval is very important to children. Adults who grew up without parental approval often develop dysfunctional lifestyles, attempting to find approval elsewhere. Encouraging your children with lots of approval helps them understand the unconditional love God shows to us in Jesus.

441 Express your pride. Say, "I am so proud of you because you overcame your fear of sleeping in the dark. No parent ever had a greater child. You are a beautiful gift from God." There is a difference between approval of a child's behavior and feeling proud of your child because of good behavior. People can approve of others without necessarily being proud of them. Find ways to show your children how proud you are that they are living out Christian values in their lives.

442 Ask your child what you could do to make him or her as happy as you are. If possible, do what your child suggests. Link emotional affirmation to demonstrating positive values. Sometimes parents think they are reinforcing Christian values when their children actually don't care for the activity. My friends Joyce and Stan took their children on a weekend camping trip. At the camping site there was boating, swimming, a tire swing, fishing, and outdoor barbecues. The children were bored and kept asking why they couldn't watch television or play video games. Finally, Joyce and Stan packed up and went home, frustrated and upset with their children. Their children were glad to be home. One went to visit a friend. Another spent a couple of hours playing a video game, and a third watched sports on television. Joyce looked at Stan and grinned, "Oh, well! You win some and lose some. Next time we'll know what to plan."

443 Tell your child all the reasons you are thankful for him or her. Explain that your love is not contingent upon behavior, but that your pride in your child grows when you see personal growth in positive directions. Say, "When I see you sharing your toys with a friend, I realize how proud I am of you for sharing Jesus' love." "When you told me how you stood up for your friend at school today, I realized what a good friend you are and how proud I am of you."

444 Give spiritual affirmation to your child by praying aloud during family devotions and thanking God for your child and the way he or she has lived out your values. You might pray, "God, You saw Danny this week when he told the truth at school about not doing his homework. You knew it was hard for him to tell the truth when he could have said he lost it on the way to school. But You helped him know what was honest, and he made the best decision. I am so glad to see You at work in Danny's life to help him be an honest boy. I am so proud of him. Thank You."

445 Find a Bible verse that affirms the value your child has demonstrated. Read it aloud together, then write the date of the behavior you are rewarding in the margin next to that verse. For example: When Ben is honest, read Colossians 3:9. When Shana helps with chores without complaining, read Philippians 2:14. When Tommy confronts a friend in a kind way to resolve a mutual problem, read Ephesians 4:15. When Betsy expresses anger but resolves the problem before doing something unkind, read Ephesians 4:26–27. When Chris is cheerfully obedient, read Ephesians 6:1. When Lily demonstrates her love by doing kind deeds, read Philippians 1:9. When Josh learns that Jesus will help him do anything he needs to do, read Philippians 4:13.

446 As a reward tell your child to pick any activity he or she wants to do and the whole family will participate in that activity. (You do reserve the right to veto dangerous or inappropriate activities.) Get the whole family to participate. You may be surprised at just how much fun you can have doing things you would never have chosen to do.

447 Tell your child you want to affirm that he or she can pick one of the house rules to be relaxed for one day. (Again, you retain veto rights, but be as flexible as you can.) It won't hurt your child to have dessert first at one meal, eat a few treats, stay up late one night, or have friends over to spend the night on a school night just once.

448 Give your child verbal feedback that what he or she did was awesome. Be lavish but believable with your praise. Kids like to hear that they are amazing to you or that you think they are awesome.

You may note that your child has an awesome memory (for some things, not necessarily for homework or the jacket that keeps getting left at school!), ability to figure things out, sense of organization, understanding of words, insight into other people, or sensitivity to others. Let your child know what you see that is truly unique, special, wonderful, and totally awesome.

449 Make a chart with your family members' names down the left side and the values you wish to reinforce across the top. "Catch" one another living out your values and put a sticker or star in the appropriate square on the chart. (No fair filling in your own square!) When someone has an entire row of stars, plan a family celebration. Thank God for the fruit of the Spirit evident in that individual.

450 Display a Blessing Tree on your kitchen table. Anchor a small branch in a flower pot with soil or clay. Your children will enjoy using a small artificial Christmas tree during the Advent and Christmas seasons. Each evening say a special prayer for one family member. Let everyone share how that person has been a special blessing during the week. Decide on a value that the honored individual has demonstrated. Write that value and the individual's name on a suitably shaped piece of construction paper (heart, star, cross, fruit, etc.). Hang the shape on the tree with yarn or string.

451 When your children tell you about a time they acted upon their Christian values, show your appreciation by applauding. Retell the story at dinner so the whole family can applaud and affirm with you. Sing a song of praise to God together.

452 Make a crown from construction paper or cardboard and foil to reward a significant incident when your children demonstrate Christian values. Pray with them, thanking Jesus for loving them so powerfully and promising to give them a crown of life in heaven.

453 Make simple thank-you notes decorated with stickers or markers. Each week, have your family think of one friend, caregiver, teacher, church staff member, or professional person who has demonstrated a Christian value. Write a thank-you note to that individual.

454 Design symbols—heart, cross, dove—for values important to you. Reproduce these symbols as patches that can be attached to your children's jackets, jeans, or shirts.

455 Design a badge of courage. When your child lives out his or her faith in a courageous way, pin on the badge. Pray together, thanking God's Holy Spirit for keeping your child's faith strong and for giving him or her the courage to express this faith.

456 Design a bumper sticker that affirms a value demonstrated by your children. Write "My child is an honest person" or "My child demonstrates self-control." Use masking tape to put the sticker on your car's bumper.

457 Give your child a commemorative certificate to celebrate an incident when he or she lived out your Christian values. You can buy blank certificates in stationery stores or make one on your computer. Frame the certificate and hang it in your child's bedroom. Share with your child times you first noticed him or her living out his or her faith through demonstrating positive values.

458 Place a Servant Jar on your kitchen table. Family members may place coins or cash in the jar when they feel they want to give a thank offering to Jesus. When the jar is full, use the money to buy groceries for your church's food pantry or a homeless shelter.

459 Print a computer generated banner and post it in your home to announce the accomplishments of your children.

460 Put notes in your children's lunches telling them how great a decision they made, how proud you are of them, or affirming them for personal growth you have noticed in a specific value area.

461 When you buy your child a new outfit, talk about how God forgives our sins because of Jesus and dresses us with His love.

462 Write a song about your child and his or her accomplishments in learning and demonstrating a positive value. Sing it to your child during dinner.

463 Write a poem to your child celebrating his or her success in demonstrating loving values.

464 Dedicate a song on the radio to your child in thanks for his or her choice to demonstrate Christian values in behavior, words, and actions. Be sure your child hears the dedication. Some radio stations will make a tape of the dedication and the song, which your child can keep as a souvenir.

465 Send your child a greeting card expressing how you feel about his or her faith.

466 As your children grow older, periodically ask them to clean their closets and place outgrown clothes and toys no longer used in a box. Together, take the donations to your church for distribution or to a shelter.

467 Make a campaign button with your child's photo on it and the value you want to affirm.

468 Label a box "Hide-and-Seek Awards Center." Fill it with construction paper, scissors, stickers, and markers. When family members notice an individual demonstrating a Christian value, they can make that person an award and hide it in a place where that individual will discover it.

469 Develop a perpetual accomplishment chart for each child. At the top write the child's name in large block letters. Begin numbering accomplishments in a listing under the name. List accomplishments that demonstrate physical, intellectual, social, and spiritual growth—learning to tie shoes, forgiving brother, etc. Keep numbering year after year. Imagine your child accumulating more than 1,000 accomplishments over a period of several years.

470 Write a tribute to your child and post it in a conspicuous place in the house. Use flowery language, gush, be creative. Remember this is a way to celebrate your child's living out values you have taught, so emphasize behaviors that demonstrate this in the tribute. You might have the tribute printed with a fancy font on a large poster so your child can have it as a keepsake.

471 Make a large felt banner celebrating a particular issue, decision, or value important to your children. You can work on this as a family, or make the banner yourself and present it to your children. Use appliqués, glue and glitter, liquid embroidery, and your imagination. Display the new banner for at least a week in the living room or family room. When friends visit, they can be told the significance of the banner.

472

Give your child a balloon bouquet with the values you appreciate in him or her written on the balloons.

473

When your child demonstrates a positive value by behaviors or choices, make it a point to call and share the incident with grandmother, uncle, aunt, cousins, and your adult friends who know your child. Be sure your child "overhears" you making the telephone calls. This lets your child know how much you appreciate what you are observing in his or her life. Another way to communicate this message to your child is to comment over dinner, "I told my friend Margene about you today. I told her how you …"

474

Give thanks for the growth of your children's faith-life when you pray at church or during your home Bible study. This progress is most appropriate to celebrate with the family of believers. If your children are there, be careful not to embarrass them by what you say. Let your children know that you thank God daily for the way they are living out their faith.

475

Write new words to an easy, popular tune ("Happy Birthday" will do) that celebrate a special decision, choice, or value demonstrated by your child. Then send your child a singing telegram.

476

Give your child a Bible with his or her name inscribed in gold on the cover. Before you present the Bible, underline or highlight special verses that speak about the values your child is exemplifying. Read these verses with your child and pray together, asking the Spirit's guidance in continuing to live out the faith.

477

During a school vacation, have one child come to work with you (if this is allowed). Introduce your child to your co-workers. Take your child to lunch and talk with him or her about what you do at work and how proud you are to share this with him or her. Tell your child what qualities you see in him or her that would make a good employee.

478

Spend time alone with your child on an adventure he or she would enjoy. A train trip to the next town, an hour alone on the lake in a rented boat, climbing to the top of a hill or mountain, a scuba lesson, or a tandem parachute jump are some examples of the types of adventures children might find terrific.

479

Set up an appointment with a Christian adult—pastor, sports figure, professional person—your child admires. Tell the person you are asking for a short meeting because your child admires him or her. Explain that you hope this meeting will be an inspiration to your child, helping him or her to see the importance of sharing faith in every walk of life.

480

Give your child something of yours that he or she has long admired but which has been a "hands off" item. This might be a favorite sweater, pen, mirror, wallet, blanket, picture, tool, piece of jewelry, or perfume. Explain that you are giving something you truly value to your child because you truly value the way he or she is sharing Jesus' love.

celebrate together

"At this moment, I find being a parent unbelievably joyous," Patrick told his family with a happy smile. They were eating dinner at their favorite restaurant as a family celebration. His 7-year-old son, Sean, had just received a Bible from his Sunday school teacher for memorizing 25 Bible passages. As soon as Patrick saw Sean's delight in the gift, he announced, "This is a very special day. Let's all go out to dinner!"

PATRICK AND HIS WIFE, Marilyn, are good at finding things to celebrate together as a family. They give parties, take special trips, send thank-you notes, and find other creative ways to celebrate positive expressions of Christian values. Celebration is a way to underscore the spiritual development and other milestones in the lives of your children. It is a way of sharing joy together. One reason to celebrate is to cause your children to associate positive feelings with having made a decision or choice consistent with values you want to reinforce.

"I'm really angry," 12-year-old Mike told his mother. "I think my teacher is wrong. She wrote on my referral slip that I did not try to do my math in class. I did try. I am mad, very mad!" Although expressive, he didn't raise his voice. "And I told her that I thought she was being

unfair and that her referral was not true. I didn't yell at her or anything. I just let her know it hurt me to have her accuse me of something I wasn't guilty of."

Lynn, Mike's mother, was so busy preparing supper that she merely nodded, making a comment here and there as he poured out the whole story. That night as she prepared to go to bed, Lynn realized that Mike had made a breakthrough. She wondered how she could have not picked up on this immediately. Teaching Mike to deal with anger had been one of her major challenges in recent months. She had talked about ways to confront people calmly, had role-played with him, and had modeled dealing with her own anger so he could see how it could be done. They had prayed together that God would give Mike a chance to demonstrate self-control in a difficult situation. Lynn wanted to wake her son and shout for joy. But she waited.

The next morning at breakfast Lynn complimented Mike for being able to voice his anger to his teacher and to tell her about the incident. "I'm so proud of you!" Lynn said, smiling happily.

"I know. Guess God answered our prayer, huh?" Mike responded offhandedly as if such a milestone were an everyday occurrence. "Do we have any jelly for the toast?" Lynn passed the jelly, still, smiling.

This kind of breakthrough calls for a family celebration. You would want to underscore it, highlight it, mark it, and make it a memorable milestone for your child.

Don't have celebrations every day. Keep them for the really special moments. Too-frequent celebrations become routine and their power to motivate children will be diminished. Here are a few celebration ideas.

481

Take out an advertisement in your local newspaper. Make it at least 2″ high and a column wide. Be careful not to embarrass your child by the advertisement or you will defeat the purpose of the celebration. Don't use last names or initials. Be sure to include "Mom and Dad," "Mom," or "Dad." Use generic language, but be sure that you let your child know what it is you are celebrating. Examples of generic language might be: "Way to go, Aaron!" "Kathy, we're proud of you, Mom and Dad." "Craig is an amazing young man." "Nancy has a big fan club." "Congratulations, Matt." "Peggy just reached a milestone. Hurrah!"

When the paper comes, open it to the ad, circle the ad, and lay it beside your child's breakfast or dinner plate. You may want to help your child frame the ad or include it in the family celebration scrapbook.

482

Host a party to celebrate one of your children. This is not a birthday party or a holiday party. It is simply a time to show how much you appreciate the values you see in your child. You might have each guest write one thing to appreciate about your child on a slip of paper. Place all the slips in a bowl. Take turns drawing a slip of paper and reading aloud what was written. Mixing up the slips and reading them as they are drawn protects the anonymity of the guest who wrote that particular tribute. This saves embarrassment for both your child and the guest.

Have guests relate stories about your child that demonstrate positive values. Decorate a cake with a positive affirmation for your child, such as "You behave in kind, loving, and generous ways" or "Thanks for sharing your love with us."

483 Have a party to celebrate values you embrace as a family. Decorations for the party might include posters with specific values on them. You could serve cookies with values written on them with icing. During the party, focus on the values and how different family members demonstrate those values in their lives. You might work together to cut out magazine pictures and words to make a collage reflecting the values demonstrated by your family.

484 Have a party to celebrate a major decision your child has made that is in line with the values you have been teaching.

485 Allow each child to invite a friend to join your family for a favorite outing. This might be going to an amusement park, river rafting, hiking, whale watching, skiing, or inline skating. Be sure your children know that the reason you are willing to pay for their guests is because you appreciate the personal growth you have seen in each child. Be specific when you tell them this. Don't just say, "I want to do this for you because I'm proud of you," unless you follow that up with "because the other day I noticed that you ..." You will need to tie the celebration to specific behaviors or choices your children have made that demonstrate they are living out their faith.

The outing need not be expensive but must be something special that you don't normally do. And you must participate in the outing also. Don't just be an observer or chauffeur for the children. This is your act of celebrating with your children and you need to take an active part in the experience. When you return home, pray together, thanking God for the good time and looking forward to the celebration you will one day have in heaven.

486

Take the family on a hot air balloon ride combined with a picnic. This may be expensive, but it is also an activity that not all their friends will have experienced, so it would be quite special. Perhaps you can find a family rate or an off-season rate.

487

If cost is of little concern to you, then do something spectacular such as having a pilot skywrite a message of congratulations to your family. Or make a banner that celebrates your family to be flown behind a small aircraft. The message might read, "Join the Peterson family in celebrating honesty (or some other value)!"

488 Celebrate church festival days as a family. Send one another flowers on Easter. Bake a birthday cake for Jesus at Christmas.

489 Design a T-shirt for your family that celebrates your values. Then buy T-shirts or sweatshirts and silk screen the design onto the shirts. Giving your children the shirts is one option. Doing the silk screening together as a family is a better option. It may be messy and even frustrating, but as you work together, you can discuss why it is important to you that these values be a part of each family member's faith life.

Wear the shirts and go out for pizza together. Take a picture of your family wearing the shirts. Months later, tell "remember when we made the family shirts together" stories. In this way you will keep the celebration memory alive.

490 At a very special point in your children's development, plan a week-long celebration with different activities for each day. The last day culminates with the "super bowl" of all celebrations. For example:

- **Sunday:** Prepare a dinner that has two of each child's favorite foods. (Don't worry if the menu doesn't make sense! It's only one meal. Anything goes.)

- **Monday:** Make felt banners.

- **Tuesday:** Place advertisements in the local newspaper.

- **Wednesday:** Send balloon bouquets.

- **Thursday:** Silk screen T-shirts.

- **Friday:** Have a family game night.

- **Saturday:** Take friends on a major outing or have a celebration party.

Decorate the house for the celebration. Make your house look like a political campaign headquarters with crepe paper, balloons, posters, pictures, hats, etc. Each day add more decorations to those already up.

Have a parade down your street. Make floats using bicycles, cars, wagons, tricycles, strollers, or any other means of transportation you have. Wear costumes. Play recorded band music. Include neighbors who want to participate. Make large banners to carry that say, "(Your last name) Family Celebration." At the end of the parade, grill hot dogs for everyone.

Once or twice a year, take the family to a nice restaurant you usually cannot afford. Make the evening a wonderful celebration where each family member is recognized for living out positive values. Recount the incidents that demonstrate spiritual growth by your children (and by parents).

Take the family to a nice hotel with a swimming pool, whirlpool, exercise room, music in one of the public areas where children are welcome, and other amenities you don't have at home. Check in one afternoon and spend part of the next day playing tourist by visiting places of interest you haven't yet seen. Enjoy the hotel during the evenings. Have a nice dinner. Sleep in or get up early and enjoy what the hotel has to offer.

494

Plan a "This Is Your Life" evening for one of your children. Ask relatives and friends to prepare personal vignettes that illustrate the values in your child's life. Remember funny experiences and relate them as part of the program. Prepare a special photograph album for pictures taken at the program. Have the entire evening videotaped for lasting memories.

495

Take a cross-country vacation as a celebration. When Darcy graduated from high school, her parents, Doug and Donna, told her they would take a graduation trip as a family to anywhere in the world she wanted to go. She picked a place she had always wanted to see. This may be beyond your price range, but you can make any trip special.

496

When you make a major purchase for the family (for example, car, large-screen television, swimming pool), use the occasion to plan a family celebration. The first time you enjoy the purchased item, thank

God for all His physical and spiritual blessings. Plan a special thank offering to take to church the next Sunday.

497

Have a family evening when you appreciate one another. Complete the following sentence for each family member: "I see Christ in you when …" This is more than a celebration, it is an affirmation that your children are becoming conformed to the image of Christ (Romans 8:29).

498

Have an all-night party for your children (only if they are older than 9 or 10). Allow each child to invite a friend. Watch videos, play board games, surf the Internet, pop popcorn, make fudge, tell jokes, play video games, take turns playing your favorite music, or plan some other fun activity. End up with a big breakfast and get some sleep!

499

Name a star after your child. You can do this by paying a fee (approximately $50) to an organization such as the International Star Registry, 34523 N. Wilson Road, Ingleside, IL 60041. The telephone number is (847) 546–5533. You will receive a hand-embossed certificate stating the star has been named for your child. (Note: There is some controversy about whether the star is "officially" named because these organizations are not recognized by the scientific community.) When you look at the stars at night, thank God for His blessings more numerous than stars and thank your child for being a special blessing to you.

500

Have a graduation ceremony for your child when you believe he or she has truly accepted and lived out some of the major values you are teaching. Give your child a diploma for graduating from the "Having to Be Reminded School." You can rent a cap and gown and play a recording of "Pomp and Circumstance" if you like. Serve tea and cookies at the graduation reception following the ceremony. Make the celebration fun, unusual, and memorable.

501

Ask your minister to prepare a short service of thanksgiving to celebrate your child's growth in the life of faith. Invite your minister and his family to dinner. Use the best china, serve sparkling cider in champagne flutes, and prepare your child's favorite foods (even macaroni and cheese looks elegant on china!). After the meal, ask your minister to lead the gathering in the special service. Give a copy of the service to your child for his or her values scrapbook. (Before planning this event, speak with your child. The object is not to embarrass, but to celebrate.)

never give up hope

WHEN I HAVE felt discouraged as a parent, when I have felt as though I am the biggest failure because my children have made choices I can't accept as right, I have been comforted to remember that I am in good company. Think of the parents in the Bible who had children whose values they could not accept.

- Adam and Eve's firstborn son killed his brother in a jealous rage. How they must have grieved over Abel's death and Cain's curse.

- Eli, a priest in the house of God, had two sons whose values were totally unacceptable to God.

- King David had a son named Absalom. As a young man Absalom had his servants kill his brother Amnon. Rightfully afraid of David's wrath, Absalom fled the country. Five years passed before David saw or spoke to his son. When he did, they were reconciled. But Absalom, far from being grateful, spent the next 40 years trying to undermine his father's authority in Israel. During that time God's Word says Absalom "stole the hearts of the men of Israel." Finally, Absalom launched a successful rebellion, usurped the throne, and moved into a tent on top of King David's home, forcing David to flee for his life. When David prepared his battle plan, he ordered his generals to deal gently with Absalom. The soldiers disobeyed and Absalom died. When David heard the news, he was heartbroken and cried, "Oh my son, Absalom, my son, my son. Would God I had died for you!" His son was more than 60 years old at this time and had spent many years in rebellion against his father, yet David still mourned his death. David must have wondered how a son of his could have chosen such a destructive value system.

As I think about these parenting "failures," I take comfort in the fact that God loved me and my children enough to have given His own Son's life for us. He forgives my failures and sins just as He forgave the sins of His Old Testament children in the promise of Christ.

When I have had moments of joy at seeing signs of maturity in my sons, I think of the biblical parents who rejoiced in their children.

- How proud Bathsheba must have been when her son, Solomon, pleased the Lord and became the wisest ruler of his time.

- How thrilled Hannah must have been when she saw Samuel, the son she had begged the Lord to have, grow up into a wise servant of God.

You, too, are in good company. It is the company of all parents who love their children and sincerely want to teach them scriptural values. Some days you will rejoice, and some days you will mourn. Then one day you will get to be a grandparent and discover once more how much joy a child can bring. As one man said, "If I knew grandparenting was so much fun, I'd have done it first!" Good idea, but it doesn't work that way. First, we must parent. So learn to enjoy the parenting experience and the opportunities to teach Christian values to your children.

Don't expect results overnight. Positive and lasting results don't come quickly. But God is faithful, and you will see hints of what your children are becoming in Christ and of the positive values they are learning to model. Those flashes of maturity are wonderfully encouraging to us all.

Like many other parents, I clung to Proverbs 22:6, "Train a child in the way he should go, and when he is old he will not turn from it." And I prayed over Proverbs 10:1b, "A wise son brings joy to his father, but a foolish son grief to his mother." My prayer has always been, "Lord, make me a wise mother and teacher and help me rear wise sons."

I think that the principle of 1 Corinthians 3:6–8 applies to our efforts in teaching our children values. Paul is talking about how some people receive the Gospel. He says that sometimes one person plants the seed, another person waters, but it is God who gives the harvest. God's Holy Spirit placed faith in my sons' hearts. As a mother, I asked God to help me plant the seeds of Christian values. Others in my sons' lives added to what I started, and I trusted God to bring my sons to the place where they would choose biblical values and make Christ-like choices. I could do no more. I am thankful God can.

Pray faithfully, communicate, explain, explore, model, teach, and reinforce your values with your children. Then celebrate the joys your children bring to you, to others, and to God.

Well done, thou good and faithful parent!